GOOD PROSE

TRACY KIDDER & RICHARD TODD

GOOD PROSE

The Art of Nonfiction

RANDOM HOUSE *New York*

Published in the United States by Random House, an imprint of
The Random House Publishing Group, a division of Random
House, Inc., New York.

RANDOM HOUSE and colophon are registered trademarks of
Random House, Inc.

LIBRARY OF CONGRESS CATALOGING-IN-PUBLICATION DATA
Kidder, Tracy.
Good prose : the art of nonfiction / Tracy Kidder and
Richard Todd.
p. cm.
Includes bibliographical references and index.
ISBN 978-1-4000-6975-0
eBook ISBN 978-0-679-60472-3
1. Authorship. 2. Prose literature—Authorship. 3. Creative
nonfiction—Authorship. I. Todd, Richard. II. Title.
PN145.K466 2013
808.02—dc23   2012021165

Printed in the United States of America on acid-free paper

www.atrandom.com

246897531

FIRST EDITION

Book design by Simon M. Sullivan

To Chris, Sammy, Nick, and Maddie,
and to Tommy, Jamie, Theodore, and Penny

Our doctrine is, that the author and the reader should move along together in full confidence with each other.

ANTHONY TROLLOPE, *Barchester Towers*

CONTENTS

CONTENTS

INTRODUCTION

===

We met in Boston, at the offices of *The Atlantic Monthly*. Neither of us can remember the date, but it must have been around the time our first joint effort as writer and editor was published, in July 1973.

By then *The Atlantic* was 117 years old. You sensed lineage when you walked up to its headquarters, an old brownstone on the corner of Arlington and Marlborough streets, facing the Public Garden. It was prime real estate, but it was also in Boston, not New York or Los Angeles. This was a magazine headquarters that seemed to say it was untouched by commerce, like the wealthy Boston matron who, in an old joke, says, "We don't *buy* our hats, we *have* our hats." A boiler room clamor faintly tolled in the offices upstairs, which had achieved High Shabbiness: faded mementos on the walls, layers of discolored paint on the ornate moldings, threadbare carpeting. The building once, in the era of Silas Lapham, had been a single-family mansion, and much of the floor plan had survived—many small rooms in back, in what must have been the servants' quarters, and in front, offices with fireplaces that editors used now and then when the Boston winter outperformed the heating plant.

It was an era that in memory seems closer to *The Atlantic*'s distant past than to our present, an era of typewriters and secretaries—mostly young, wry women with first-class educations trying to find their way into publishing careers. There were a few older women, two of them editors; one wore a hat at her desk. The women of both ranks kept regular hours. The men arrived midmorning and not long afterward went to lunch. "I'm going to grab a sandwich," the editor-in-chief, Bob Manning, would tell his assistant, as he headed for the all-male sanctuary and full luncheon menu of the Tavern Club. The more junior men stepped out soon afterward, and often ended up at the Ritz Bar, a block away on Arlington Street. An editor with a writer in tow could charge his lunch to the magazine. Eggs Benedict, a couple of small carafes of white wine, and back to work, rarely later than two thirty. Many afternoons were cheery.

The Atlantic was more or less broke by then, just barely paying its expenses and about to become an exercise in cultural deficit spending for its owner. Editors didn't earn much, less than twenty thousand a year (which bought more then than now, of course, in part because there weren't as many things to buy). A young writer was paid by the piece, two or three thousand dollars at most for a long article that might take four months to complete.

The Atlantic's archives held a trove of articles and stories and poems by just about every major American writer of the late nineteenth and early twentieth centuries. The magazine was still one of America's preeminent cultural arbiters, but the role was increasingly hard to play. In politics, *The Atlantic* had long stood for liberal thought. Now its editors stared out their windows onto a world in which liberalism was under attack from both sides, from the Weathermen as well as the Nixon White House. Every month the staff argued over the magazine's cover and usually ended up with something colorful and overstated, in the vain hope that a touch of sensation would improve news-stand sales. But the covers threatened the magazine's cultural legitimacy, the real attraction for its true audience and for many who worked there.

•

Nearly forty years is long enough to make the "us" of back then feel like "they." We were young—Kidder twenty-seven, Todd thirty-two—and each of us was trying to stake out a liter-ary future. To Todd, editing at *The Atlantic* granted prestige, like owning a fine antique. If he'd been in charge, the magazine would have reverted to the monochrome covers of its heyday.

As for Kidder, the idea of publishing articles at *The Atlantic* was more than exciting enough, since he would have been grate-ful to be published anywhere. Phone calls were expensive back then and allowances for research miserly. For a young writer short of funds, it was convenient to spend time in the building, camping out as it were in one of its many vacant back offices and using the magazine's phones for long-distance calls to sources for articles. Kidder spent many days and quite a few nights in the building, and many hours working with Todd, whose office had a fireplace and a view. After-hours provisions could be found in the bar in Manning's office down the hall.

We called each other by our surnames, as our sergeants had in army basic training. To Kidder, a childhood for Todd seemed improbable—he must have been born old, and probably born ironic to boot. To Todd, and practically everyone else, Kidder was young beyond his years. He was plainly ambitious, but his self-esteem ranged from abject to grandiose. Once, at a Christmas party that went on too long, he confronted Bob Manning and announced, "I'm the best damn journalist in the Western Hemisphere." Hung over and contrite the next morning, he was comforted by Todd, who said, "At least you didn't claim the whole world." Each imagined himself forbearing of the other.

Kidder wrote and rewrote many versions of his first *Atlantic* article, about a mass murder case in California. He had imagined the piece as a sequel to *In Cold Blood*. At some point Bob Manning sent the manuscript back to Todd, having scrawled on it, "Let's face it, this fellow can't write." Todd kept this comment to himself and merely told Kidder that the piece still needed fixing, and the rewriting continued.

A long association had begun. Todd knew only that he had a writer of boundless energy. For Kidder, to be allowed not just to rewrite but to rewrite ad infinitum was a privilege, preferable in every way to rejection slips. And for Todd, it was possible to imagine that a writer willing to rewrite might turn out to be useful. Todd once remarked to a group of students, never expecting he would be quoted, "Kidder's great strength is that he's not afraid of writing badly." The truth was that Kidder was afraid of writing badly in public, but not in front of Todd. Kidder would give him pieces of unfinished drafts. He would even read Todd passages of unfinished drafts, uninvited, over the phone. Very soon Todd understood when he was being asked for reassurance, not criticism, and would say, "It's fine. Keep going." When a draft was done, Todd would point out "some problems," and another rewrite would begin.

That ritual established itself early on and persisted through many articles and Kidder's first two books. A time came—midway through the writing of *Among Schoolchildren*, about a fifth-grade teacher—when Kidder began revising pages before Todd had a chance to read them. This was a means of delaying criticism forever. No doubt that was Kidder's goal, and he could remain happily unaware of it as long as he kept on rewriting. Things went on that way for a while, until Todd said, in the most serious tone he could muster, "Kidder, if you rewrite this book again before I have time to read it, I'm not working on it anymore." Kidder restrained himself, and the former routine was reestablished.

Eventually *The Atlantic* changed hands. Its book publishing arm was sold off, its headquarters relocated, its old building renovated into a corporate office. We lingered for a time, working under a new head editor, William Whitworth, who was to both of us exemplary. He once told Kidder, "Every writer needs another set of eyes." When Todd moved on to do his own writing and to edit books, Kidder followed him.

This book is in part an account of lessons learned, learned by a writer and an editor working together over nearly forty years. *Good Prose* is addressed to readers and writers, to people who care about writing, about how it gets done, about how to do it better. That you can learn to write better is one of our fundamental assumptions. No sensible person would deny the mystery of talent, or for that matter the mystery of inspiration. But if it is vain to deny these mysteries, it is useless to depend on them. No other art form is so infinitely mutable. Writing is revision. All prose responds to work.

We should acknowledge some other predispositions. We're sticklers on fact. Nonfiction means much more than accuracy, but it begins with not making things up. If it happened on Tuesday, that's when it happened, even if Thursday would make for a tidier story. (And in our experience, at least, Tuesday usually turns out to make for a more interesting story.) This is not to confuse facts with the truth, a subject we will deal with.

We also believe in the power of story and character. We think that the techniques of fiction never belonged exclusively to fiction, and that no techniques of storytelling are prohibited to the nonfiction writer, only the attempt to pass off inventions as facts. We think that the obscure person or setting can be a legitimate subject for the serious nonfiction writer. And we think that every piece of writing—whether story or argument or rumination, book or essay or letter home—requires the freshness and precision that convey a distinct human presence.

During the past three decades American culture has become louder, faster, more disjointed. For immediacy of effect, writers can't compete with popular music or action movies, cable network news or the multiplying forms of instant messaging. We think that writers shouldn't try, that there is no need to try. Writing remains the best route we know toward clarity of thought and feeling.

Good Prose is mainly a practical book, the product of years of experiment in three types of prose: writing about the world, writing about ideas, and writing about the self. To put this another way, this book is a product of our attempts to write and to edit narratives, essays, and memoirs. We presume to offer advice, even the occasional rule, remembering that our pronouncements are things we didn't always know but learned by attempting to solve problems in prose. For us, these things learned are in themselves the story of a collaboration and a friendship.

GOOD PROSE

1

BEGINNINGS

═══════

The first time I worked with Todd was over the phone. We talked about the article I was trying to write. The conversation went like this:

What was wrong with the article? I asked.

Well, first of all, he said, and he paused, as if perhaps he was sorry to have to say this. Well, first of all, the first sentence.

I had wanted a spectacular opening. My first sentence read: "In the spring of 1971, someone went mad for blood in the Sacramento Valley." A fellow student at the Iowa Writers' Workshop had praised that sentence. Todd didn't like it?

No, he said, it was melodramatic.

Reminded of this conversation decades later, Todd said with a touch of irony, which I hadn't heard in his voice back then: "Well, I guess I stand by that judgment."

—TK

To write is to talk to strangers. You want them to trust you. You might well begin by trusting them—by imagining for the reader an intelligence at least equal to the intelligence you imagine for yourself. No doubt you know some things that the reader does not know (why else presume to write?), but it helps to grant that the reader has knowledge unavailable to you. This isn't generosity; it is realism. Good writing creates a dialogue between writer and reader, with the imagined reader at moments questioning, criticizing, and sometimes, you hope, assenting. What you "know" isn't something you can pull from a shelf and deliver. What you know in prose is often what you discover in the course of writing it, as in the best of conversations with a friend—as if you and the reader do the discovering together.

Writers are told that they must "grab" or "hook" or "capture" the reader. But think about these metaphors. Their theme is violence and compulsion. They suggest the relationship you might want to have with a criminal, not a reader. Montaigne writes: "I do not want a man to use his strength to get my attention."

Beginnings are an exercise in limits. You can't make the reader love you in the first sentence or paragraph, but you can lose the reader right away. You don't expect the doctor to cure you at once, but the doctor can surely alienate you at once, with brusqueness or bravado or indifference or confusion. There is a lot to be said for the quiet beginning.

The most memorable first line in American literature is "Call me Ishmael." Three words, four beats. The sentence is so well known that sometimes, cited out of context, it is understood as a magisterial command, a booming voice from the pulpit. It is more properly heard as an invitation, almost casual, and, given the complexity that follows, it is marvelously simple. If you try it aloud, you will probably find yourself saying it rather softly, conversationally.

Many memorable essays, memoirs, and narratives reach dra-

matic heights from such calm beginnings. *In Cold Blood* is remembered for its transfixing and frightening account of two
murderers and their victims, and it might have started in any
number of dramatic ways. In fact, it starts with a measured descriptive passage:

> The village of Holcomb stands on the high wheat plains
> of western Kansas, a lonesome area that other Kansans call
> "out there." Some seventy miles east of the Colorado border,
> the countryside, with its hard blue skies and desert-clear air,
> has an atmosphere that is rather more Far West than Middle
> West.

Although a bias toward the quiet beginning is only a bias, a
predisposition, it can serve as a useful check on overreaching.
Some famous beginnings, of course, have been written as grand
propositions ("All happy families are alike . . .") or sweeping
overviews ("It was the best of times . . ."). These rhetorical gestures display confidence in the extreme, and more than a century of readers have followed in thrall. Expansiveness is not
denied to anyone, but it is always prudent to remember that one
is not Tolstoy or Dickens and to remember that modesty can
resonate, too. Call me Ishmael.

Meek or bold, a good beginning achieves clarity. A sensible
line threads through the prose; things follow one another with
literal logic or with the logic of feeling. Clarity isn't an exciting
virtue, but it is a virtue always, and especially at the beginning
of a piece of prose. Some writers—some academics and bureau-
crats and art critics, for instance—seem to resist clarity, even to

write confusingly on purpose. Not many would admit to this. One who did was the wonderful-though-not-to-be-imitated Gertrude Stein: "My writing is clear as mud but mud settles and the clear stream runs on and disappears." Oddly, this is one of the clearest sentences she ever wrote.

For many other writers, writers in all genres, clarity simply falls victim to a desire to achieve other things, to dazzle with style or to bombard with information. With good writing the reader enjoys a doubleness of experience, succumbing to the story or the ideas while also enjoying the writer's artfulness. Indeed, one way to know that writing deserves to be called art is the coexistence of these two pleasures in the reader's mind. But it is one thing for the reader to take pleasure in the writer's achievements, another when the writer's own pleasure is apparent. Skill, talent, inventiveness, all can become overbearing and intrusive. And this is especially true at the beginnings of things. The image that calls attention to itself is often the image you can do without. The writer works in service of story and idea, and always in service of the reader.

Sometimes the writer who overloads an opening passage is simply afraid of boring the reader. A respectable anxiety, but nothing is more boring than confusion. In his introduction to *The Elements of Style*, E. B. White suggests that the reader is *always* in danger of confusion. The reader is "a man floundering in a swamp," and it falls to the writer (whose swamp of course it is) to "drain this swamp quickly and get his man up on dry ground, or at least throw him a rope."

Clarity doesn't always mean brevity, or simplicity. Take, for example, the opening of Vladimir Nabokov's memoir *Speak, Memory*:

The cradle rocks above an abyss, and common sense tells us that our existence is but a brief crack of light between two eternities of darkness. Although the two are identical twins, man, as a rule, views the prenatal abyss with more calm than the one he is heading for (at some forty-five hundred heart-beats an hour). I know, however, of a young chronophobiac who experienced something like panic when looking for the first time at homemade movies that had been taken a few weeks before his birth. He saw a world that was practically unchanged—the same house, the same people—and then re-alized that he did not exist there at all and that nobody mourned his absence. He caught a glimpse of his mother waving from an upstairs window, and that unfamiliar ges-ture disturbed him, as if it were some mysterious farewell. But what particularly frightened him was the sight of a brand-new baby carriage standing there on the porch, with the smug, encroaching air of a coffin; even that was empty, as if, in the reverse course of events, his very bones had disintegrated.

There is nothing confusing about this paragraph, but it does invite us to engage with a sinuous idea, and it introduces an au-thor who asks our fullest attention. He expects long thoughts from us. The invitation is clear and frank, and it is delivered with a shrug: accept it if you will.

•

You can't tell it all at once. A lot of the art of beginnings is deciding what to withhold until later, or never to say at all. Take one thing at a time. Prepare the reader, tell everything the reader needs to know in order to read on, and tell no more. Journalists are instructed not to "bury the lead" (or "lede," in journalese)—instructed, that is, to make sure they tell the most important facts of the story first. This translates poorly to longer forms of writing. The heart of the story is usually a place to arrive at, not a place to begin. Of course the reader needs a reason to continue, but the best reason is simply confidence that the writer is going someplace interesting. George Orwell begins *Homage to Catalonia* with a description of a nameless Italian militiaman whose significance is unknown to us, though we are asked to hear about him in some detail. At the end of a long paragraph of description, Orwell writes:

> I hoped he liked me as well as I liked him. But I also knew that to retain my first impression of him I must not see him again; and needless to say I never did see him again. One was always making contacts of that kind in Spain.

It seems strange to begin a book with a character who vanishes at once, when the first few sentences suggest that we are meeting the book's hero. In fact, the important character being introduced is the narrator, who seems a man of great particularity and mystery of temperament. We don't know much about him, and we want to know more. We're ready to follow him.

What happens when you begin reading a book or an essay or

a magazine story? If the writing is at all interesting, you are in search of the author. You are imagining the mind behind the prose. Often that imagining takes a direct, even visceral, form: who *is* this person? No matter how discreet or unforthcoming writers may be, they are present, and readers form judgments about them. Living in an age when authors hid behind the whiskers of third-person omniscience, Thoreau wrote: "We commonly do not remember that it is, after all, always the first person that is speaking." Readers today do commonly remember that. They may remember it to a fault. The wise writer, while striving to avoid self-consciousness, remains aware of the reader's probing eye.

The contemporary author Francine du Plessix Gray offers a provocative way to imagine encounters between writer and reader: "A good writer, like a good lover, must create a pact of trust with the object of his/her seduction that remains qualified, paradoxically, by a good measure of uncertainty, mystery and surprise." The heart of this advice, the tension between giving and withholding, identifies a narrative decision that faces all writers, though in emphasizing Eros, Gray seems to overlook the true romance of writing. The "mystery and surprise" can be genuine, shared between writer and reader, rather than calculated.

One morning a piece of wisdom comes over National Public Radio, in an interview with a jazz guitarist who remembers working with the great Miles Davis. The guitarist recalls that Davis once advised him how to play a certain song: "Play it like you don't know how to play the guitar." The guitarist admits that he had no idea what Davis meant, but that he then played the song better than he ever imagined he could. "Play it like you don't know how." Cryptic advice, but a writer can make some sense of it: Don't concentrate on technique, which can be the same as concentrating on yourself. Give yourself to your story, or to your train of ideas, or to your memories. Don't be afraid to explore, even to hesitate. Be willing to surprise yourself.

And so there is trust of another kind at work. At some point you must trust yourself as a writer. You may not know exactly where you are going, but you have to set out, and sometimes, without calculation on your part, the reader will honor the effort itself. In Ghana, once a British colony, where English remains the official but a second language, they have an interesting usage for the verb "try." If a Ghanaian does something particularly well, he is often told, "You *tried*." What might well be an insult in American English is high praise there, a recognition that purity of intention lies at the core of the achievement. The reader wants to see you trying—not trying to impress, but trying to get somewhere.

2

NARRATIVES

===

STORY

For me, finding a story that I want to tell has always depended less on effort and method than on what my college teacher the poet and great translator Robert Fitzgerald called "the luck of the conception." Luck of this type may begin with a chance encounter, a suggestion from a stranger, a sudden notion that seems like grace descending. I know nothing more thrilling than the arrival of a good idea for a story. The problem is that good ideas seem to arrive on schedules of their own, and are sometimes disguised as bad ones.

I once had an idea for a book that came from my experience of having bought an old house and having tried to fix it up myself. The constructed landscape changed for me; for the first time I looked at buildings and saw craftsmanship or the lack of it. A few years later, I was able to hire a team of carpenters, admirable craftsmen, who straightened out some of the messes I had made. My idea was to write a book largely about them. Home-building in America would be the general subject, and the story would follow the carpenter-builders on some sort of construction project yet to be identified.

I tried this idea on editors, agents, writer friends. No one liked it. So I gave it up and spent nearly two years looking into other possibili-

ties. Todd suggested a book about a captain of industry, but I managed to arrange just one interview, on the top floor of a New York City skyscraper. The CEO told me he didn't think he could afford to be written about, because he didn't want the world to know how little he actually accomplished. I wrote a few articles about atmospheric chemistry and chemists, but no roads opened onward for me. I went out west, thinking I might write a book on wilderness, but when I tried the idea on Bill Whitworth, at The Atlantic, he said, "Is this just going to be more beautiful writing about beautiful places?" Finally one day I said to Todd, "You know, I'd really like to try to write that book about carpenters."

I remember that he looked at me quizzically, as if to ask why I hadn't told him this before. "Well, do it then," he said.

I ended up following not just the team of carpenters but all the principals involved in the building of a single-family house. The research took about a year. And then, my notes assembled and indexed more or less, I retired to my office to try to begin to make sense of what I had observed. I imagine that this moment is much the same for most nonfiction writers. We sit at desks in our offices, apart from the world, gazing at those notebooks stacked on our tables, hoping there are stories in them but once again unsure.

At those times I have usually heard worrying voices, and partly to quiet them, partly to forget myself, I have started writing in haste, without much of a plan. But this time was different. I actually felt calm. I sat gazing out the window, listening, I swear it, to the book I wanted to write. What I heard was something like the sound of my mother's voice reading Dickens, for me the sound of an old-fashioned novel. Then I started to write, and I seem to recall that I had been writing quite happily and steadily for about six months when I went *to a cocktail party, where a new acquaintance asked me what I was working on. After I told him, he said, "You mean you're writing a whole book about the building of a house?"*

Ordinarily I would have been upset. But by then I felt sure there was a good story accumulating in my draft. It seemed to be opening in many directions, and I was fascinated by the architect and builders and incipient homeowners, and by the sometimes stormy relations among them. It was a ménage à trois without sexual connotations, a story about craftsmanship and social class, a multidimensioned story. I could probably get this naysayer interested, I thought, but only if I told him the whole thing, and that would take too much time and effort. And besides, just then, for once, I wanted to keep it all on paper and in my head.

I tend to worry now when a story is easily summarized and in summary sounds interesting or, even worse, exciting. This may be superstition, but I believe there is one sure dictum about judging one's material, a cocktail party rule so to speak: it isn't always a bad sign when a potential story doesn't talk well.

—TK

Every story has to be discovered twice, first in the world and then in the author's study. One discovers a story the second time by constructing it. In nonfiction the materials are factual, but the construction itself is something different from fact.

Some writers begin by spending only a day or two making up the barest outline, the barest guess as to the essential elements of their story, and then they start trying to tell it, taking every turn that seems promising. The approach has advantages. It's like learning a route by driving it rather than memorizing the map. The danger does not lie in making mistakes (it's good to make them early) but in committing too soon to a promising conception that may be hard to abandon when it proves unworkable. Conversely, some writers deliberate for days, weeks, (months!) on end, until they feel sure of their plan. But you can never know if you understand your story until you try to tell it. There is a middle ground—to proceed with enthusiasm but to leave yourself a way out: to write in blocks of prose without dwelling on where the blocks will go and the connections among them. In the end, you have to try to find the method that works best for you, remembering that most writers do solve this problem and that how one solves it doesn't matter at all to the reader.

It helps of course to have an idea of what you are looking for. What, after all, is a story? It is not a subject. A good story may include a great deal of information on any number of topics or issues. It may blossom with implications. It may be a way of seeing a world in a grain of sand. But that grain of sand can't be just any grain of sand. A story lives in its particulars, in the individuality of person, place, and time.

There are many archetypal stories: narratives of quest and trial, sin and redemption, identity and self-sacrifice; narratives of the chase, the mystery, the love triangle, the struggle between good and evil; narratives in which trouble is averted, escape is achieved, tragedy happens. Many, maybe most, nonfiction writers go looking for narratives with those silhouettes, and they feel lucky when they find the real thing, because stories out in the world don't usually turn out as expected. Even a story that has already happened, a story that a writer sets out to reconstruct, isn't always as dramatic as it first appears. The villain isn't quite as villainous as he looked in his photograph; the warring parties settle the lawsuit in midtrial; the murder wasn't a murder after all. Nonfiction writers, especially ones new to the factual narrative, are vulnerable to those sorts of disappointments. "I don't have a book," the young writer says when the events don't deliver the kind of obvious drama in which everyone recognizes a story. But usually what's missing isn't a story. What's missing is a broader way of thinking about what makes for a good story.

It is a misleading truism that drama comes from conflict. Conflict in stories is generally understood as an external contest between good guys and bad guys. But to say that *Hamlet* depicts the conflict between a prince and usurper king is (obviously) to oversimplify that rich, mysterious drama, indeed to misunderstand it completely. The most important conflict often happens within a character, or within the narrator. The story begins with an inscrutable character and ends with a person the author and reader understand better than before, a series of events that yields, however quietly, a dramatic truth. One might call this kind of story a narrative of revelation.

In Jon Krakauer's *Into the Wild*, a young man goes to Alaska with a head full of romantic notions about living in the wilderness and ends up starving to death. Told straight up, this story might have made for a ghastly adventure yarn. Krakauer's troubling and poignant version allows us to see the young man and, through him and his plight, to view afresh the great American subject of wilderness.

In Anne Fadiman's *The Spirit Catches You and You Fall Down*,

American doctors and Laotian Montagnard immigrants tangle over their wildly different understandings of a child's case of epilepsy. This is the central action of the story, an external conflict about a child's welfare. But the essence of the story resides in the growth of understanding and sympathy between the two camps, with the author in the background learning something too.

A Civil Action, by Jonathan Harr, also relies heavily on an event-driven narrative, the story of an environmental lawsuit. To some of the author's friends, this had seemed like a dubious premise. Who would care to read a book about another environmental scandal in which the villains were predictable, the larger meanings all too clear? But the events turned out to be a personal saga, not an allegory. The main character was attempting a good deed, but he was also eccentric, driven, and ambitious. As a lawyer, he was willing to take his fight far beyond the legally rational. His character drove him to achievement, and it also landed him in a mess. In other words, *A Civil Action* and *The Spirit Catches You* and *Into the Wild* are all at their deepest levels narratives of revelation.

Revelation, someone's learning something, is what transforms event into story. Without revelation, a story of high excitement leaves us asking, "Is that all?" Discovering the deeper drama of revelation is a challenge for the nonfiction writer, especially the writer who has happened onto a cliff-hanger story. And it is an opportunity, also a potential solace, for the writer who has in hand a story that lacks obvious drama but that may contain other important qualities.

For a story to have a chance to live, it is essential only that there be something important at stake, a problem that confronts the characters or confronts the reader in trying to understand them. The unfolding of the problem and its resolution are the real payoff. A car chase is not required.

•

POINT OF VIEW

From the late 1970s until 2000, I worked with Kidder on five books, all but one of them written in the third person. In at least one of these, Among Schoolchildren, *the third person proved imperative. Kidder had taken no part in the proceedings, and his task was to portray a tiny corner of the world of elementary-school education largely as it appeared through the eyes of a teacher. He accomplished this by observation and intensive after-action interviews with the teacher, in which the essential questions were, "What were you thinking then?" and sometimes, "What are you thinking now?"*

The third person was a less obvious choice in some of Kidder's other books, but he stuck to it, I think, partly out of a love of the neatness and discipline of the thing—stuck with it until the early 2000s, when he wrote Mountains Beyond Mountains. *He began his first draft of that book in the third person, but the plan quickly fell apart.*

The central figure in the story, Dr. Paul Farmer, was not (not then, anyway) particularly famous. Yet he was not an ordinary man either. His capacities were extreme, his actions heroic, his selflessness saintly. What he needed—needed as a character, that is—was to be made credible. Larger-than-life figures seem to need life-size translators. Kidder's initial third-person descriptions of Farmer fell flat. Who was this guy who sleeps three hours a night and spouts pronounce-

ments about social injustice? He seemed otherworldly. He cured the sick, sure, but could you stand to be around him? As we talked about this issue, Kidder insisted that on the personal level, Farmer was wonderful to travel with, courteous and funny and interesting. "And when you get sick, he takes care of you," Kidder added. But how to make the man as palatable to readers?

What Kidder realized finally was that he had to be a stand-in for the skeptical reader, he had to present himself as a person of ordinary limits in endurance and sympathy, who could be in the company of a saint and live to tell the tale. Thus Kidder for the first time portrayed himself, registering the discomfort and diminishing skepticism that he had felt while traveling with Farmer.

In the first section of the book, Kidder arrives at the doctor's oasis-like hospital in the desperately poor Haitian countryside. He describes Farmer with wary admiration and then takes a long walk with him into the hills, in pursuit of a patient who needs treatment. The doctor, though suffering from various maladies himself, climbs effortlessly. The author flags. But that (though actual) is a sort of stage business. What really matters is that Kidder provides a way for us to hear Farmer, as if his high pronouncements were coming through our own earthly skeptical ears. They reach the summit, have the meager reward of a Life Saver candy, and then Kidder recounts the scene as they gaze down at the impounded waters of a dam that has drowned the land of countless peasants and relegated them to extreme poverty. And Farmer says, "To understand Russia, to understand Cuba, the Dominican Republic, Boston, identity politics, Sri Lanka, and Life Savers, you have to be on top of this hill."

Kidder doesn't respond to Farmer, but says to us: "The list was clearly jocular. So was his tone of voice. But I had the feeling he had said something important. I thought I got it generally. This view of drowned farmland . . . was a lens on the world. His lens. Look through it and you'd begin to see all the world's impoverished in their billions and the many linked causes of their misery. In any case, he seemed to think I knew exactly what he meant, and I realized, with some irritation, that I didn't dare say anything just then, for fear of disappointing him."

One of the side effects of saints is that they can make the rest of us feel crummy, or even annoyed. Here the author gets annoyed for us. "With some irritation" is the crucial phrase in the passage. One can imagine the effect if the account were recast in the third person, as in newspaperese: "Farmer said to a reporter . . ." The scene without the management of the self-revealing narrator would be meaningless or even absurd.

This is more than convenience, and what happens in microcosm is a model for the whole book. The author's understanding of the subject becomes the story. Paul Farmer is revealed to us through the growing comprehension of the narrator. This is another example of the narrative of revelation.

—RT

Point of view is the place from which a writer listens in and watches. Choosing one place over another determines what can and can't be seen, what minds can and can't be entered. The choice also deeply affects the tone, the author's apparent attitude toward the events and people of a story—an element of storytelling that is easiest to spot when it goes wrong and the reader senses, for instance, that the author is condescending toward a character but doesn't seem to know it. Point of view is a place to stand, but more than that, a way to think and feel.

The main choice of course is between the third and first person, between a disembodied voice and "I" (in nonfiction synonymous with an aspect of the author). For some, the choice is made before sitting down to write. Some writers feel obliged to use the third person, by tradition the voice of objectivity, the disinterested mode of address appropriate for the newspaper or for history. Other writers, by contrast, seem to adopt the first person as a reflex, even if they are not writing autobiographically. But choosing a point of view really is a choice, fundamental to the construction of nonfiction narratives and carrying serious consequences. No moral superiority inheres in the first or third person, in their many varieties, but the wrong choice can deaden a story or distort it enough to turn it into a lie, sometimes a lie composed of facts.

One thing to consider is the scale of the story. Take, for instance, the opening of *There Are No Children Here*, by Alex Kotlowitz:

> Nine-year-old Pharoah Rivers stumbled to his knees. "Give me your hand," ordered his older brother, Lafeyette, who was almost twelve. "Give me your hand." Pharoah reached upward and grabbed hold of his brother's slender fingers, which guided him up a slippery narrow trail of dirt and brush.
>
> "C'mon, man," Lafeyette urged. . . . "Let's go." He paused to watch Pharoah struggle through a thicket of vines. "Man, you slow."

The two boys are climbing up a railroad embankment, looking for both adventure and relief from summer in the housing
projects of Chicago. A third person hovers over this scene, an
observer, but at least on first reading, we don't think about that
person. The observer could have revealed himself, reported perhaps on how he skinned his own knees following the boys. But
even though we know he's there, he remains invisible. To some
readers, telling a story this way makes the story incomplete. But
if Kotlowitz had revealed himself in this small opening scene, he
would have had a lot of explaining to do, about his relation to the
two boys and his bona fides and so on, and besides quite possibly
boring most readers, all that information would have ruined the
scale of the story's beginning. It would have enlarged the field of
vision and made the boys and their world smaller than Kotlowitz
wanted them to seem. He wanted to invite us into the boys' cir-
cumscribed landscape. He wanted to tell their story as much as
possible from their perspective. A first-person narrator would
have ruined the spell that Kotlowitz wanted to create, the readers' illusion that they are alone with the boys.

So the size of the world that a writer is trying to create often
has something to do with the presence or absence of the word
"I." Against a large background, "I" can provide human scale.
Most travel writing, for instance, depends on the first person,
the figure in the photograph that shows you just how tall the
statue is. As a rule, the smaller the canvas, the more intrusive
the first person is likely to be.

Even a complex story with multiple characters can be made
more immediate by the absence, not the presence, of a first-
person narrator. The disembodied voice of the third person can

sometimes allow for greater intimacy with the subject than the first person, as in this passage from *A Civil Action:*

> The lawyer Jan Schlictmann was awakened by the telephone at eight-thirty on a Saturday morning in mid-July. He had slept only a few hours, and fitfully at that. When the phone rang, he was dreaming about a young woman who worked in the accounting department of a Boston insurance firm. The woman had somber brown eyes, a clear complexion, and dark shoulder-length hair. Every working day for the past five months the woman had sat across from Schlictmann in the courtroom, no more than ten feet away. In five months Schlictmann had not uttered a single word directly to her, nor she to him. He had heard her voice once, the first time he'd seen her, but he could no longer remember what it sounded like. When their eyes had happened to meet, each had been careful to convey nothing of import, to make the gaze neutral, and to shift it away as quickly as possible without causing insult.
>
> The woman was a juror. Schlictmann hoped that she liked and trusted him. He wanted desperately to know what she was thinking. In his dream, he stood with her in a dense forest . . .

Thus begins the introduction to the main character of a non-fiction book. We're put in bed with him. Actually, we're asleep with him, not just watching him dream but watching his dream with him. Critics and writers have a term for this technique, a term other than chutzpah. They call it the "restricted third person" or the "limited third person." The reader sees the world as the character sees it. This mode seldom appears in pure form. More often we see what the character sees, but also see the character seeing it. It's a technique more common in fiction, of course.

In nonfiction, the restricted third person has practical costs. The right to use it has to be earned; one can write "she thought" or "he dreamed" only if the person has confessed to the thoughts or the dreams, and only if the writer has good reasons to believe the accounts are true. Jonathan Harr spent eight years writing *A Civil Action*—some of them wasted in devising ways not to write, as he happily admits, but many of them spent in keeping company with his main character, ears and eyes and notebook open during the many times when nothing important was happening. Spending more time with a subject than most writers could afford or tolerate seems the only sure way of building the kind of relationship that can let a writer into someone else's dream life.

When to prefer the first person to the third? You would almost certainly choose it if you were involved in the events you're describing, and you would probably feel obliged to choose it if your presence had a knowable effect on the outcome. Choosing the first person can also be more nearly a matter of convenience than honesty. "I" can simply seem the more natural mode, and, in that slight sense only, more honest, less artificial. The involvement of the first-person narrator can be very light indeed. Sometimes "I" is there just to facilitate the movement of the piece: "We met in a nondescript café on the Lower East Side . . ." Or simply to register what is said: "He told me that he came to places like this because they reminded him of Budapest before the war . . ."

A variety of the first person is available for this role. One might call it the "first-person minor," or the "restricted first person," or the "reasonable person." The distinguishing characteristic of this point of view lies in the limits and strictures it places on itself. As a rule, not much about the narrator is revealed, including the narrator's opinions.

The first-person minor has been around for some time. It has long flourished at *The New Yorker.* You can pick it up already well established sixty years ago, with Lillian Ross and her classic profile of Ernest Hemingway—who, within range of Ross's notebook, reveals himself to be in a punch-drunk (and plain drunk) state of defiance. Its marvelously, almost parodically urbane first line reads: "Ernest Hemingway, who may well be the greatest living American novelist and short-story writer, rarely comes to New York." The profile feels intimate, and the author does nothing to hide her presence, and yet she manages to seem unobtrusive. She assumes a rather dutiful persona. She appears when Hemingway summons her. We hear nothing of her life. If you stop reading and think about it, you realize that this might have been quite a moment for her, a writer in her early twenties who was profiling the world's most celebrated author. A candid personal journalist could have made herself into a figure of high drama. Instead Ross makes herself seem like a stock figure of the time, the "gal Friday," cheerful, omnicompetent, without apparent needs of her own.

Another *New Yorker* writer, John McPhee, has characteristically written in the first-person minor. In his hands, the limited first person, while remaining indistinct in personality, can take an active hand in things, and by acknowledging his presence, and even the effect of his presence, can help illuminate the subject. The following is a brief scene from McPhee's book-length profile of Bill Bradley, called *A Sense of Where You Are*. McPhee wrote it when Bradley was a basketball star and not yet a senator. McPhee is watching Bradley practice, and Bradley misses a shot:

> . . . the ball curled around the rim and failed to go in.
>
> "What happened then?" I asked him.
>
> "I didn't kick high enough," he said.
>
> "Do you always know exactly why you've missed a shot?"
>
> "Yes," he said, missing another one.
>
> "What happened that time?"
>
> "I was talking to you. I didn't concentrate. The secret of shooting is concentration."

This is a utilitarian first person. It's natural and casual, and it helps readers to see. But sometimes the reportorial first person plays a larger role, not merely useful but vital, as in profiles where the writer must take the measure of a story's characters. Do they require an identifiable set of eyes to interpret them for the reader, to manage the reader's reactions to them? There are moments when the first person ought to be restrained, others when the "I" is necessary as a gauge.

A somewhat revelatory first person lies on the wide continuum between the first-person minor and what might be called the first-person major. In some cases, it may seem necessary to reassure the reader about the accuracy of a story, and one solution may be a first-person narrator who reveals, even if indirectly, how the story was reported. At the extreme, of course, the author's gradual understanding of the subject becomes the heart of the narrative. This often happens in books about places: Bruce Chatwin's *In Patagonia*, Ian Frazier's *Great Plains*.

In his essay "Breakable Rules for Literary Journalists," Mark Kramer praises journalists who tend to present themselves with an "intimate voice, frank, human, and ironic." But this kind of intimacy is a highly stylized thing. To put it directly, the narrative "I" is a fiction. This is not to say it is a lie. It is an emblem of a personality made up of elements that the author may in fact possess or may only aspire to. As in fiction, the "I" of reportage is a constructed thing, a vast simplification of its creator.

Sometimes the "I" is really out there on the page, self-dramatizing, very present indeed. Sometimes it is the "I" of personal participation in great events or dire social conditions: Mark Twain learning his way around the mining camps of the West, in *Roughing It*. More recently, it's David Foster Wallace having adventures on a cruise ship or Barbara Ehrenreich describing her taste of life as a minimum-wage worker.

Then there is the interesting case of the late Norman Mailer. He said that his book *Armies of the Night*, originally begun as a magazine article for *Harper's*, was "history as novel" and "novel as history." It seems like neither. It looks a lot like reportage, reportage that transforms the first person into the third. This is the book in which Mailer becomes "Mailer," a character covering and participating in the March on the Pentagon in 1967. At moments, his deployment of the third-person-first-person feels like a prison break. You feel the liberation in it, the possibilities it opens up to be free of the oppressive "I." The stance he affects could scarcely be more personal or more revealing, but at the same time it preserves a comic distance from the self. It is both wildly egotistical and grandly self-mocking. It might not have been possible to bring it off at all if Mailer hadn't already made himself, through his earlier work and his outlandish (and on one occasion criminal) behavior, a public figure whom plenty of people referred to as "Mailer," and not in the kindest way.

In fiction, another variation is possible, the "unreliable narrator." We are meant to understand such narrators in a different way than they understand themselves. This would be a hard act to pull off in nonfiction. But one writer has come close: the late Hunter Thompson, who presents himself as a drug-and-alcohol-crazed, hallucinating madman, driving a red rental car across the desert, on the first page of *Fear and Loathing in Las Vegas:*

> We were somewhere around Barstow on the edge of the desert when the drugs began to take hold. I remember saying something like "I feel a bit lightheaded; maybe you should drive. . . ." And suddenly there was a terrible roar all around us and the sky was full of what looked like huge bats, all swooping and screeching and diving around the car, which was going about a hundred miles an hour with the top down to Las Vegas. "Holy Jesus! What are these goddamn animals?"
>
> Then it was quiet again. My attorney had taken his shirt

off and was pouring beer on his chest, to facilitate the tan-
ning process. "What the hell are you yelling about?" he
muttered . . . "Never mind," I said, "It's your turn to drive."
I hit the brakes and aimed the Great Red Shark toward the
shoulder of the highway. No point mentioning those bats,
I thought. The poor bastard will see them soon enough.

In Thompson, hyperbole and fantasy don't masquerade as objective truth but describe the inner life of a hallucinating "I."
Thompson stretches the boundaries of nonfiction, maybe to a
point where they ought to be stretched now and then.

Characters

The attempt to render characters in a piece of writing, to create
the illusion that people are alive on a page, is so essential to
storytelling, and so dependent on every other aspect of the art,
that it can't help but seem diminished by the standard term
"characterization." That word might better be limited to perfunctory efforts. Examples of these are abundant, in fiction and
in many sorts of nonfiction. Here is one, from *Game Change*, the
most popular political book of a recent season:

The Obama brain trust—David Axelrod, the hangdog
chief strategist and self-styled "keeper of the message";
David Plouffe, the tightly wound campaign manager; Robert
Gibbs, the sturdy, sharp-elbowed Alabaman communications
director; Steve Hildebrand, the renowned field operative be-

hind the campaign's grassroots effort in Iowa—was a worry-wartish crew by nature.

Journalists who have to get a book written before its topic is stale may not have time to do more than this, to depict people as dolls or "action figures," quickly and easily understood. And moving stick figures around can be enough to give a narrative shape and dramatic action, and these, along with information and especially insider information, are all that many readers expect, or require, or even want. Great writers remind us that more is possible. Here, for example, is how George Eliot introduces the heroine of *Middlemarch:*

> Miss Brooke had that kind of beauty which seems to be thrown into relief by poor dress. Her hand and wrist were so finely formed that she could wear sleeves not less bare of style than those in which the Blessed Virgin appeared to Italian painters.

These sentences begin the book's opening paragraph, which is long by modern standards but does a lot of work. By its end Miss Brooke's plain manner of dress has become not only a means of suggesting her physical beauty, but also an entrance to her family history, her social station, the character of the place where she lives, and, on top of that, her tendencies of thought and her ambitions and a suggestion of the risks that they carry. We are promised that if we come along, we will receive much more than the simple story of what will happen to Dorothea Brooke. The lure is those hands and wrists of hers, set off by her plain sleeves. We are given just enough material to begin to imagine her in a place and situation, and the invitation to follow her is beguiling and suggestive enough that we, like many former generations of the reading "we," are inclined to accept.

More than any other aspect of storytelling, the successful rendering of characters depends on the reader. The goal is to get characters off the page and into the reader's imagination. When this happens, transport follows. We readers travel in our chairs, beds, sofas, our living rooms, our carrels in the library, to a place in our minds where we aren't quite aware that we are reading, where we wish we were like the protagonists or we say to ourselves, "Oh, God, that could be me," where we speak to the characters—"No! Don't do that!"—just as if those people were really here with us right now.

One might say this feat was easier in George Eliot's time than it is today, when many other storytelling media can do the imagining for us. But they thus limit the range of possibilities—one reason that good books rarely get turned into good movies; the Captain Ahab we imagine when we read *Moby Dick* probably doesn't look exactly like the Ahab any other reader imagines, and he certainly doesn't look like Gregory Peck. When it comes to creating the illusion of human beings in stories, writers of fiction and nonfiction still have the distinctive and necessary task of getting the reader to do the necessary work of imagining.

Some general truths apply. For instance, one sure way to lose the reader is trying to get down everything you know about a person. What the imaginative reader wants is telling details. Characters can emerge in long descriptive passages, as in Tolstoy, but brevity can also work. Graham Greene rarely gives us more than a detail or two—a face "charred with a three days' beard" or a pair of "bald pink knees"—and Jane Austen often gives us less than that, and yet the people those writers create have come alive for generations of readers.

Whether it is brief or lengthy, mere description won't vivify a statue. What we want are essences, woven into a story in moments large and small. A character has a wart. You could describe it in detail, but the reader would probably see it more clearly if you described not the wart but how the character covers it when he's nervous.

Or take the small matter of a character's age. It's a bad idea, categorically bad, to offer it via a tired pretext: "She looked a decade younger than her seventy years." Nor do you want to tack her age onto her name, as in a news story. Instead, think of a character's age not as an obligatory but as a potentially significant fact. Wait for the moment when we need to know her age in order to understand an event in the story. Or, if her age has no narrative importance, slip us the number quietly at the moment when, if you were reading, you would need it for the picture of the woman that is forming in your mind.

There are multiple ways of presenting characters. Some people will go a long way toward defining themselves through their own speech. Others may talk volubly but without revealing much. In all cases, diligent reporting produces more quoted material than a book or article can hold. Selection is necessary, and, a more delicate matter, authorial management. Take for instance a character who talks so colorfully that the writer has to acknowledge the fact, as in *The Earl of Louisiana*, A. J. Liebling's extended profile of the flamboyant governor Earl Long. At one point, Liebling recounts a campaign speech in which the governor tells a crowd that a political opponent wears expensive suits, then says of himself: "A four-hundred-dollar suit on old Uncle Earl would look like socks on a rooster." Liebling breaks in:

> It is difficult to report a speech by Uncle Earl chronologically, listing the thoughts in order of appearance. They chased one another on and off the stage like characters in a Shakespearean battle scene, full of alarums and sorties.

An author can also rely on others to comment for him. Liebling spends most of the first four chapters of *The Earl* relating others' stories and opinions of the governor. Point of view is a powerful tool for making people materialize in our imaginations. Characters who seem lifeless at the end of a draft can sometimes be revived by letting the reader see them through another set of eyes, or several sets of eyes, as in Liebling. Minor characters encountered in the flow of a story can function as lenses on the main characters. Minor characters can also serve as foils, the human background against which we see the main characters more clearly.

A minor character can also become a liability. Sometimes in a draft, a minor character grows dimensions and threatens to wreck the narrative scheme. It is assumed that something like this happened to Shakespeare. In *Will in the World*, his book about Shakespeare's life and times, Stephen Greenblatt writes: ". . . in an anecdote that circulated in the seventeenth century, [Shakespeare] is said to have remarked of *Romeo and Juliet* that he had in the third act to kill Mercutio—the wildly anarchic mocker of romantic love—before Mercutio killed him." Probably every serious writer, in nonfiction and fiction, has had the experience of seeing a minor character grow so vivid as to seem more important or at least more interesting than the principals of the story. It's a better kind of problem than many. Such characters are always hard to give up, but they are often diagnostic: maybe you haven't worked hard enough on the main characters, or maybe that minor character ought to be major, and if so, maybe you should ask yourself if there is something wrong with the point of view or the structure of your story.

Some minor characters who remain minor are, as E. M. Forster puts it, "flat," known in one dimension only. The type is abundant in Shakespeare's plays and in any work that includes a wide cast. Flat characters are part of the glory of Charles Dickens. The dinner guest Twemlow in *Our Mutual Friend* is an extreme example of flatness, known mainly by his resemblance to a table:

> There was an innocent piece of dinner-furniture that went upon easy castors and was kept over a livery stable-yard in Duke Street, Saint James's, when not in use . . . The name of this article was Twemlow. Being first cousin to Lord Snigsworth, he was in frequent requisition, and at many houses might be said to represent the dining-table in its normal state. Mr. and Mrs. Veneering, for example, arranging a dinner, habitually started with Twemlow, and then put leaves in him, or added guests to him.

Whether flat or multidimensional, minor or central, characters need settings in order to live. A setting can be an actual
place, but it is always more than that. Above all, a setting tells
what is at issue—what a character is trying to do, what a character fears or is trying to hide, hopes to gain or stands to lose,
what a character is up against. Depicting such circumstances
and feelings is one way you can get the reader imaginatively involved; something matters to this person on the page, and we
can imagine its mattering to us.

Sometimes what's at stake, as in a narrative of revelation, is
the author's own quest to discover a character's identity. The
challenge implicit in all biographical writing is made explicit in
these cases. In *Joe Gould's Secret*, for example, we accompany
Joseph Mitchell in getting to know an outlandish Harvard-
educated bum and in ultimately discovering the poignant lie by
which the man has lived. A. J. Liebling's essay "Quest for Mollie," less well known but no less beguiling, begins with Liebling
in the role of war correspondent reporting from North Africa.
He comes upon the body of a young American enlisted man and
hears stories about him from other soldiers: the daring, wildly
eccentric "Mollie" supposedly captured an entire regiment, six
hundred Italian soldiers, single-handedly. We return to New
York with Liebling and accompany him on his further search for
Mollie's identity, or identities.

•

Many well-wrought characters live in nonfiction, but the library of fictional characters is much larger. Nonfiction writers

spend useful time there, trying to figure out what they can borrow and, equally important, what they can't.

When we read fictional and factual narratives, we conjure up characters through their deeds: characteristic actions and contradictory actions, behavior in moments of stress, of mastery, of weakness. Suggestions of a character's motives may be implicit in the deeds, but many readers want more. We want to imagine that we know why characters do what they do and feel as they do. We want to understand characters in a story better than we understand ourselves. This, of course, is an illusion available only in fiction. The writer of factual stories is constrained by what the subject is willing and able to reveal.

Fiction writers tell us that sometimes their imagined characters seem to take over, to grow and change on the page, acquiring unexpected qualities and doing unexpected things, just as if they were alive. Fiction writers can invent ways out of whatever problems this creates; if necessary, they can always kill off the character in the midst of the story, as Shakespeare did Mercutio. Nonfiction storytellers don't have that option.

In nonfiction, events and characters stand in paradoxical relation to each other. There is a fundamental difference between writing about a man who gets into an accident and writing about the accident. The event is the event. It happened. It's a fact. As for the man, no one knows for sure who he really is, what skein of motives and desires led him to this event. And yet he, not the accident, is your fixed star. Once you have selected a person to write about, that person has become the central mystery you want to solve, knowing that you never will solve it completely.

In your research, you spend all the time and perspicacity you can muster on that man. Eventually, you grasp a vision of him in the round, a vision that honors his variousness. Then you try to re-create that vision in writing, presenting him through things you've seen him do, things you've heard him say, things you've heard others say about him. You choose those things from among many candidates in your notes, selecting them partly because they seem interesting or colorful or funny in themselves, but mainly because they express your vision of the character. It may be that when you met him, the man thought of his accident as the most important thing in his life. But suppose nothing about the accident enhances or complicates or expresses your sense of who he is. You can't invent another, more revealing accident for him to be in, but you can choose *not* to write about the real one. The honest nonfiction storyteller is a restrained illusionist.

STRUCTURE

Things happen in time, and time is crucial in storytelling. Kidder and I once established a rule: you can mess with chronology, but you have to have a good reason to do so. This is one of those empty propositions that can have a good effect, this one as a check against the deliberate scrambling of narrative time, a gambit very appealing to some writers, but frustrating to readers when it is not employed in service of the story.

Our rule was put to the test with Kidder's Strength in What Remains. *The book recounts the life from boyhood to middle years of a*

man named Deogratias, a native of the east central African country
Burundi. The basic story contains many powerful and, at least superficially, improbable events: Deo's escape on foot, first from civil war
and then from the Rwandan genocide; the painful reconstruction of his
life and psyche in New York City (Deo slept for some months in Central Park); the resumption of his education (at Columbia University);
and ultimately his return to Burundi as an American citizen, intent
on helping with the reconstruction of his native country.

Although the events were all in the past, the story was nonetheless
heavily reported. Kidder revisited the scenes of Deo's travail, spending
time with him in New York and Boston, interviewing people who had
helped him, and traveling with him to Burundi and Rwanda.

All this research in hand, how to tell Deo's story? This became a
problem of both point of view and time. Our solution had two parts.

Kidder's first draft roughly honored the chronological rule. It had
wonderful moments, but as a whole it was unsatisfying. The chronology asked a great deal of the reader. Specifically, it asked American
readers to sit still for an account of a painful childhood in a place most
had certainly never heard of. (I did not have to imagine this
ignorance—Deo was my introduction to the very existence of Burundi.) Another option was to start with the most dramatic moment,
the harrowing story of Deo's escape, but this would have committed the
old theatrical crime of starting too high. Where would we go from
there? Moreover, the reader wouldn't have much reason to care about
Deo, not having met him in less extreme and more familiar circumstances. Yet another possibility might have been to hew strictly to the
order in which Kidder reported the story. This is often tempting and
almost always a mistake. At crucial moments the presence of the narrator would have served only to mute the drama. How the narrator

would ultimately appear was a problem to be solved, but this was clearly not the narrator's story.

With the comfort of a rough draft to remind us that we had a book, that it was just a matter of getting it right, we set about giving the story a new structure. We determined that it would be a good idea to get Deo to New York as soon as possible. But then how would we get him back to Burundi, and where would the narrator be?

It was a summer day on the coast of Maine, the sort of afternoon when weather and season invite you not to be urgent about anything, but we were feeling urgent about this. We sat in silence for some time on the porch of Kidder's cottage. I found myself sketching out a plan on a yellow pad. After a while Kidder said, "Well, this is all I've come up with," and held up his own yellow pad. I smiled and held up mine. The drawings were identical—four arrows coming in from the left-hand margin, interleaved with four arrows coming in from the right. Kidder said, "We've been doing this too long."

But we were pleased, once we realized that we were indeed thinking of the same thing. In the first part of the book, Kidder would create two alternating chronologies, each moving straightforwardly in time. One chronology would begin with Deo's departure from Burundi and take us through his time in New York. The second would recount his youth in Burundi, culminating in his narrow escape from war and genocide. This second chronology would end where the first began, and, as it turned out, it could end on a line that Deo remembered clearly, a line that would by that time, with Deo's sufferings in New York already told, be nicely ironic: with the consular official in the US embassy in Burundi handing Deo a visa and saying, "Good luck in New York." Some other refinements suggested themselves as we talked. The New York sections would get progressively shorter, the Burundian sections longer. And it was plain that the narrator had no useful presence: the story would be told in the third person through Deo's perceptions—that is, it would be told in Kidder's words mostly, but they would describe Deo's memories.

I suppose the book could have ended there. But much was left over from Kidder's reporting trips. The original purpose of these had been to understand and verify Deo's story, to gather detail firsthand. But the results went far beyond sights and sounds and smells: portraits of the people who had come to Deo's aid in New York, and Kidder's observations while traveling in Burundi. In seeing Deo revisit places of trauma, Kidder also witnessed some of its effects. He had the sometimes heartbreaking privilege of watching a man deal with ungovernable, tormenting memories. We wanted to find a form for these experiences, too, for Kidder's first-person observations. We decided that a prologue would be the best way to establish the fact of a first-person narrator. But many pages told from Deo's point of view would intervene. How to bring the narrator back? After a while it seemed there was no advantage in doing this other than boldly.

In effect we decided that the story should be told twice. After 145 pages, the reader comes upon Part Two, and the disarming phrase with which the author steps onstage for the first time since the prologue: "I first met Deo in Boston, about a decade after he had fled Rwanda and Burundi." Part One would be told through Deo's eyes, Part Two through the author's. This yielded many benefits. Much that got in the way in the rough draft—the observations Kidder had made during reporting, observations which did not come from Deo—now became useful. And Part Two, in allowing the reader to see how the author reported the story, worked to dispel any doubts a reader might have about the story's credibility. Most important, retelling the story in the first person helped the reader see (and in candor it helped author and editor realize) what the book was really about. It was not just about extraordinary resilience and courage, but also about memory and how the mind can work to repair itself after devastating experience. This kind of thing has happened often in our years of working together. More than most writers, I think, Kidder discovers his stories by writing and rewriting them. In this case, finding the story's structure was the means to finding its theme.

So, a twice-told tale that starts near the end, interleaves two chronologies, and then the second time around is told through a different set of eyes, with a new chronology, which reenacts the author's research. Not the simplest structure imaginable (and far from the one with which the book began). For all of that, the rule for us continues to hold. Don't mess with chronology unless you have a good reason.

—RT

The fundamental elements of a story's structure are proportion and order. Managing proportion is the art of making some things big and other things little: of creating foreground and background; of making readers feel the relative importance of characters, events, ideas. Often this means upsetting normal expectations by finding a superficially trivial detail or moment that, on closer examination, resonates with meaning.

As for order, its fundament is time. Writers profit from knowing when events actually occurred. It is always a good idea to construct a detailed time line and, for some, to write rough drafts chronologically. If you know the actual sequence of your story, all the details dated in relation to one another, you avoid muddle and misunderstanding, and can write with a feeling of authority, which tends to insinuate itself into prose.

It is especially important to know a story's chronology if you are tempted to alter it. For the writer, an important tension arises between chronology and deliberate alterations of chronology. As you're writing, you ought to feel that pull. It challenges you. Do you want to tell parts of your story out of sequence in order to be arty, just to show off? Or do you have reasons that arise from your exploration of the story itself?

Serious narratives offer us good reasons for caring what will happen to the characters. Why those things happen, especially the characters' motives, is a higher order of question than what will happen next, but most stories lack propulsion if they lack sequence. Telling stories in chronological order has a distinguished lineage in Western literature, which includes, among others, all the classical narratives and most novels well into the twentieth century. One might say that the straight-ahead treatment of time reflects a moral rather than a psychological understanding of the world. In Jane Austen, characters define themselves and are judged by what they do, from present moment to present moment, event by event. We aren't told that Mr. Darcy is courting Elizabeth because of what happened to him when he was eight years old. Rather, we are asked to believe that he has an essential nature, and that we should be more interested in what it is than in where it came from. This is, after all, the frame of mind in which most human beings spend most of their waking hours.

The straightforward structure is not obsolete, even in our psychological age. Ron Suskind's *A Hope in the Unseen* dramatizes the progress of a young African American named Cedric Jennings. We meet him as a student in an inner-city high school in Washington, DC. Jennings has a gift for math, and he has a code of behavior formed by his mother's faith in him, his own faith in God, and a fierce pride. He is determined to escape the ghetto, and he does, improbably, to Brown University. In high school he is a pariah, scorned for his industry and ambition and what some see as arrogance. Things aren't always easier for him at Brown, where he is an anomaly of another sort, genuinely poor in a subsociety of mostly middle-class African Americans, passionate in an academic world that values reason and nuance, and religious among secularists. Nonetheless, he ultimately finds his place, and—the psychological engine of the book—he finds a way to adjust and also to preserve the values that got him there. Significantly for students of structure, this book, though abundant in event and detail, could not be simpler in form: a straightforward chronology, with only the smallest detours to account for Cedric's family history.

Another sort of story might fight against being told this way. Suppose that as you begin to understand your story, you sense that its deepest meanings get lost in the actual chronology, that the truth which lies in the facts depends on one event being presented before another, even though the actual order was the reverse. Doing this can enhance, not distort, a reader's sense both of the events' happening in time and of their relative importance. You don't pretend that the altered sequence was the real one. You find a way to signal that you have changed the order. One time-honored method is to begin in medias res, at a point some distance into the narrative. Later on, you go back and recount

events that came before. It's a reflexive strategy in movies strain-
ing to make banal plots seem unpredictable. But it has better
uses.

McPhee's *Encounters with the Archdruid* is a paradigm of structural complexity. It's like a piece of fine cabinetry, fussy and
great, and great in part because nothing in the writing calls attention to the structure. The book, from the early 1970s, is in
essence an extended profile of David Brower, then the nation's
most prominent and controversial environmentalist. The story
is told in three parts, each of them an "encounter" showing
Brower in confrontation or debate with people who represent for
him the forces of environmental destruction.

The final section takes place mostly on a raft trip down the
Colorado River. One could scarcely design a more perfect jour-
ney through time and space, one in which the surroundings are
a locus for the issue at hand, the uses and, in Brower's eyes, the
misuses of dams. The section begins not with Brower but with a
portrait of one of his nemeses, a man named Floyd Dominy, head
of the federal Bureau of Reclamation, whose life has been organized around the building of dams large and small. At the end of
one of his interviews with Dominy, McPhee poses this question
to him: "If Dave Brower gets into a rubber raft going down the
Colorado River, will you get in it, too?" And Dominy answers,
"Hell, yes. Hell, yes."

This is an extraordinary bit of journalistic artifice. The trip
would not have occurred under any other circumstances. It is
arranged by McPhee for McPhee's purposes as a writer. And yet,
once it is under way, the event seems utterly natural, thanks to
McPhee's stagecraft.

There are many lessons for the writer in this expedition. One of the central ones is McPhee's handling of time. The account begins in the present tense: "Mile 130. The water is smooth here. . . ." The present tense proves all too convenient for many writers. Some use what might be called the melodramatic present in an effort to engage the reader. "It's 3:00 a.m. and wolves are howling." Trying to commandeer the reader's attention in this way usually invites resistance. We find ourselves thinking, "No, it's actually the middle of an August afternoon, and I'm sitting on my back porch. Just tell your story."

McPhee inverts the formula. The trip is punctuated by heightened episodes, especially when the party is running rapids. Many writers would employ the present tense here: "Waves buffet the boat, rocks toss us in the air, spray soaks us." McPhee describes these dramatic moments in the past tense, counterintuitively but with the effect of making the rapids seem all the more daunting: "We went through it with a slow dive and climb and a lot of splattering water. We undulated. The raft assumed the form of the rapid. We got very wet. And now, five minutes later, we are as dry and warm as if we were wearing fresh clothes straight out of a dryer." He uses the same device in recounting some of the inevitable debates between Dominy and Brower. "Tonight's fight was about . . ."

Whether they are told in the past or present tense, all stories require a governing time—the present tense of the story, as it were—in which the main events occur. McPhee establishes a firm sense of his story's time by taking us some distance on the rafting trip, until we feel the pull of sequence, of the movement of the characters through time and space, and we can imagine the river and ourselves along for the ride and are wondering what will happen next. Then McPhee feels free to take us on excursions away from the river and introduce us to yet another time, a past that precedes the river trip.

At one point, the conversation turns to the river's water levels. These are controlled by the Glen Canyon Dam, upstream from the party of rafters. McPhee breaks away from the central narrative and after a visual break on the page writes:

What seemed unimaginable beside the river in the canyon was that all that wild water had been processed, like pork slurry in a hot-dog plant, upstream in the lightless penstocks of a big dam.

Then he tells us that "some days earlier" Dominy had taken him and Brower to see the dam. He dramatizes the visit, describing the place and the interaction of the two main figures there. This excursion—the recounting of another event in the midst of the main event—has important effects on the narrative, the kind of effects that justify departing from strict chronology. The digression varies the pace and enriches the texture. It also invites the reader to consider the wider context in which a small event takes place.

It is worth pausing over how McPhee manages this transition, from the river to the dam. Not the prose itself, elegant though it is, but the timing. He waits for a logical moment when he, the narrator, would be likely to remember that earlier trip. The departure is welcome, even necessary, though it is unexpected. If a story is well designed, the writer should be able to go from one subject to a rather different one, from one time to another time, without giving off a scent of arbitrariness or struggle. Sometimes two parts of a story can simply be placed next to each other and the structure fits together like one of those New England stone walls that have stood for centuries without mortar in the joints. A writer who accomplishes this might well feel gratified to hear a reader think, "I could do that. That looks easy."

3

MEMOIRS

═══════

I was sent to Vietnam in June 1968, when I was twenty-three and a second lieutenant in the army. I spent most of a year in hypothetical command of an eight-man unit, a "detachment," performing an indoor job in communications intelligence. My men and I were never in combat and came under fire only once—from mortar rounds, which landed far enough away for us to boast about the experience afterward. I should have been thankful for the safety of my assigned role, and I was, in part. But I was also acutely aware that my life in a base camp could not be called valiant.

During the first year after I came home, I told a few stories that suggested dark memories of combat. I also wrote a novel, called Ivory Fields, *the story of a young lieutenant who bore considerable resemblance to me, but who had various dramatic experiences I didn't have. No one would publish my novel. For the next fifteen years I returned off and on to the subject of Vietnam. I wrote a pair of fantastical short stories about the war, and a long article about the postwar suffering of American combat veterans, all published in* The Atlantic. *Finally, I set out to write a memoir about my own modest truth.*

I thought it might make an interesting little book. Or at least an unusual one—a memoir about a noncombatant's experience, the most common and least recorded kind of American story from Vietnam. I would make it as accurate as I could, using whatever letters and documents I had kept or could find. For the unverifiable rest, I would be faithful to my memories.

I had a problem, though. My memories embarrassed me. They weren't horrifying or tragic, but when they arrived I wanted to bury my head in a pillow. Now, as I willed myself to remember, more and more stuff came back, and as I wrote about these remembered incidents, I fell into a mode that seemed safe but was really a trap. I surrounded true stories about my earlier self with commentary from my older, wiser self, including commentary asserting that I knew I was doing this. Among the arts of self-effacement, this is elementary. It's called fishing for compliments. The book wasn't working. Giving up on it felt good, like the next best thing to finishing it.

I didn't destroy the fragmentary manuscript. I put it in a file and went back to writing about other people. Some years later I took the pages out and worked on them and put them aside again, and I did the same once more some years after that. It took me the better part of fifteen years to understand what was wrong. It was, I think, a moral problem and a technical problem. The solution to the moral one was the time it took for me to accept my intimate connection with the bumbling young lieutenant. Todd had long ago suggested a technical fix.

He had made the suggestion before I could employ it, back when I had just finished a partial first draft of my memoir. We were sitting in a booth at a restaurant. Todd was leafing through the pages. When he made a comment, I leaned across the table and wrote down what he said on the manuscript—which I still have, my transcriptions of his comments written upside down. He had come to a page on which I had quoted from my war novel, Ivory Fields, *by then a subject of comedy between us. He paused over this description of my novel's title character, a black infantryman: "Black-fire, dark-pink coals were the lips that framed the shining teeth, threw shape around the sounds, the wind that rushed between their parting."*

"I must rise to defend these metaphors!" *said Todd. He added,* "This is a novel with a theme. Its theme is its author's ambitions."

Todd had, still has, one kind of laughter to which he fully gives himself. In the aftermath, he flicks tears away from his eyes with a forefinger. When he does this, you know he has been sincerely amused. "Ivory Fields," *he said, as if intoning the name of a departed friend. Then he got serious.*

In that first draft, I had described my novel scornfully, lest the reader wonder for a moment about my current taste. Todd told me, "Play the novel for comedy. The flatter the better." *He also said, apropos of the whole story,* "Do without foreknowledge." *That is, don't set us up by trying to disown the young lieutenant. Repossess him. Or, as Todd put it at one point that evening,* "Just be there."

Todd's instructions called, in part, for irony. Not irony as mindless joking or nihilism. But irony in the older sense of saying one thing and meaning another, or of saying one thing and not saying the other. In short, irony defined as meaning more *than you say. It is sometimes a source of comedy and more generally an expression of the incongruities of life, the tricks that the world plays on us and that we play on ourselves.*

When I finally found a tolerant attitude toward my memories of myself in uniform, I thought what was silly and strange and embar-

*rassing about my behavior would be plain enough without commen-
tary. I felt that I should give up trying to place this memoir between
my remembered self and me. I should stop trying to pretend that the "I"
of the present couldn't possibly be related to the "I" who had tried, in
letters home, to suggest a picture of himself as a rugged guy who had
found his true gentleness in war—one hand holding an M16, the other
resting protectively on the shoulder of a Vietnamese boy.*

*When I first sat down to write my memoir I already had a name for
it:* My Detachment. *Fifteen years later, I felt as though I had begun
to live up to the title. Since my book was published I haven't been vis-
ited by a single one of the sudden, involuntary, stomach-turning memories from my year at war. About once a year I used to dream that I
had orders to go back to Vietnam. I haven't had that dream again.*

—TK

Memoir beckons. Although the form dates back at least to Saint
Augustine, it holds a particular allure for contemporary writers.
Ideas about privacy and decorum have changed generally; even
in daily life, Americans seem to expect more and more self-
revelation from themselves and others. Authors who would once
have felt obliged to wrap their own stories in the gauze of a
roman à clef now feel entitled, or compelled, to speak to the
reader without disguise. It feels more honest. And it can seem
beguilingly easy, at least until one tries.

"Write about what you know," writers are told, and it's logical
to conclude that what you know best is yourself. In fact, you may
know too much. In honest moments we understand ourselves as

creatures of great contrariety. Many selves compete inside. How to honor this knowledge without descending into gibberish or qualifications worthy of a chairman of the Federal Reserve? How to preside over your own internal disorder? Finding the "I" that can represent the pack of you is the first challenge of the memoirist.

Postmodern wisdom has not helped, having cast the very idea of self, any self, into doubt. In his memoir, *Self-Consciousness*, John Updike writes: "That core 'I' that we imagine to be so crystalline and absolute within us can also be attacked and analyzed as a construct that human society bestows." Updike resists this idea, with evidence that ranges from the mundane to the spiritual: the private quirks that endure through a lifetime, mingled with the sense that one also has a soul. He concludes with a definition of self that is universal and undeniable: "that window on the world that we can't bear to think of shutting."

To place yourself on the page is in part self-discovery, in part self-creation. The act feels like what a lump of clay must feel like to the hands of a sculptor. *This is all you have to work with, but you know there's a face in there somewhere.* You write a paragraph in the first person. You read it over. You meet—as if for the first time, though the face does look familiar—the person who speaks the words you have written. You think, *That's not me. This guy sounds downright mean.* You pull out his fangs. *Oh, no. Now he's getting mushy on us.* Writers want to be engaging, and it is easy to try to purchase charm at the expense of honesty, but the ultimate charm lies in getting the face more right than pretty.

Memoir, fortunately, doesn't have to take on the burden of

total self-representation. It can be confined to a time, to a relationship, to a side of one's self that doesn't pretend to encompass the whole, to a story. *Personal Memoirs of Ulysses S. Grant* is one classic example. Grant omits many important facts of his life: his drinking bouts; the means of his extraordinary rise, from working as a clerk in a dry goods store to commanding all the Union forces; his disastrous presidency; his humiliation and bankruptcy; the fact that he was writing his book in great pain from throat cancer, knowing his death was imminent. But the book is cited as one of the very few presidential autobiographies that deserves to be regarded as literature, for its lucid and dramatic account of the author's Civil War campaigns. One of Grant's biographers, Edmund Wilson, pointed out that the book has the unlikely effect of keeping the reader in suspense—"actually on edge to know how the Civil War is coming out."

Memoirs, it's said, were once the province of people like Grant, the great or at least the famous, for whom self-presentation is already an accomplished fact. Now the genre has opened, opened wide to writers with no prior claim on the reader's imagination. The current abundance of new and recent memoirs can feel overbearing, and even alarming, a symptom of spreading self-absorption. But if the democratization of the form has helped to create that oversupply, it has also produced some distinguished books. Often they tell the sorts of stories that Grant didn't tell, stories that on the surface, anyway, don't reflect kindly on themselves.

Confession as a means of reconstructing the self can have a keyhole-like fascination for the reader. Perhaps every memoir *should* reveal something the author doesn't reveal in daily life.

But confession carries various risks. A sly vanity can lurk in a recitation of misdeeds, a reveling in one's colorfulness: *Oh, what a bad girl I was!* Or one can end up presenting a much too limited concept of the self. Some, though not all, recent stories of addiction fall into this trap and leave the reader thinking, "There's more to everyone than the love of vodka."

How the writer conveys present knowledge of past experience is a delicate problem for all memoirists. The question of how much to reveal in constructing a self on the page merges into the fundamental question of how much to interpret and how much simply to describe. When to comment on the past, when simply to portray it in all its starkness and let it speak for itself? It can be tempting to disown the past only to celebrate the present self. *What a fool I was! (But how clever I am now to see it.)* And all the while the reader knows that previous selves are not so easily discarded.

Self-exploration, including confession, almost always involves other people. Some of them are bound to be offended by an honest memoir. But the good and honest memoir is neither revenge nor self-justification, neither self-celebration nor self-abnegation. It is a record of learning. Memoirs, by definition, look backward. They are one response to Kierkegaard's dilemma that life can only be understood backward but must be lived forward. Memoirs survey a past with the benefit of the knowledge that experience has yielded. With *The Education of Henry Adams*, Henry Adams created the perfect title. Every memoir worth reading could be called *The Education of the Author.* The "I" has been somewhere and it now knows something that it didn't, and that is a thing of value for writer and reader alike.

•

Here are some basic rules of good behavior for the memoirist:

- Say difficult things. Including difficult facts.
- Be harder on yourself than you are on others. The Golden Rule isn't much use in memoir. Inevitably you will not portray others just as they would like to be portrayed. But you can at least remember that the game is rigged: only you are playing voluntarily.
- Try to accept the fact that you are, in company with everyone else, in part a comic figure.
- Stick to the facts.

Stick to the facts. The words sit there in all innocent simplicity, as if sticking to the facts were no more complicated than stopping at a red light. But the facts are often at issue in memoir, and in a way that goes far beyond the fraudulent memoirs that from time to time scandalize the publishing business.

In an author's note to his memoir, *Lost in the Meritocracy,* Walter Kirn says, "There are, I suspect, a number of inaccuracies, but no deliberate deceptions." Most memoirists, struggling for accuracy, would endorse this rough code of conduct: faithfulness to fact defined as faithfulness to one's own memories. Of course, this does not entirely resolve the issue.

Like the act of remembering, the act of writing your own story inevitably distorts, if only by creating form where disorder reigns. To make sense of your life or a portion of it is to tell a story, and story often stands at odds with the ferment in which you have lived. That's one point of a story: to replace confusion with sense. The impulse of memoir is itself a fictive impulse.

What is true in macrocosm is true in microcosm. At the level of moment-by-moment rendering of the past, the factual becomes all the more problematic. One can see the problem enacted, in a brilliant form, in Frank Conroy's memoir, *Stop-Time*, a modern landmark in the genre. When the book appeared, in 1967, it became the literary equivalent of breaking news. The original dust jacket bore just two blurbs—one from William Styron and one from Norman Mailer, two of the most respected American novelists of the day. *Stop-Time* is an account of growing up rich and poor. (Conroy's mother was divorced from her well-off husband and took up with a drifter.) It was far from the first memoir about childhood, but it had a freshness and immediacy that made it seem like something new. The book served as a rebuke to the conventional sentiment that a writer ought to have achieved something in the world before presuming to write a memoir. To people who felt that way, young Conroy (and his young followers) said implicitly, *You are holding my achievement in your hands.*

An intensity of detail distinguishes *Stop-Time*, as one can see in any number of passages. Here is a scene set in a hardscrabble shack in a failed real estate development in inland Florida:

At just that moment the screen door opened and Mrs. Rawlings threw out a basin of water. It flashed through the air and struck the ground where the light spilled from the window. A thousand gleaming flies lifted from the greasy sand the instant the water hit, and fell backward the instant afterward, like a green blanket.

You don't have to read more than those few sentences to realize that you are in the company of a good writer, and when you read a succession of such sentences your appreciation is confirmed. You also may find yourself thinking about the nature of memory. When he wrote the book, Conroy was thirty, recalling events two decades past with a precision that we know the mind provides only on rare occasions. That blanket of green flies has the insistence of a memory, but did Mrs. Rawlings throw the water on that day or another, did the water land in the spot where the light spilled from the window, were the flies out that evening or on some afternoon? Does a reader care? The particulars are inconsequential, and yet it is the particulars that help to persuade us of the reality of the experience. More simply, they provide much of the pleasure of the book.

Many moments in *Stop-Time* must have been remembered in just this way, at once remembered and reimagined. These are memories that happen as they are being written. They are not fraudulent. They are completely unlike the made-up events of hoax memoir, but they are not reliably factual either.

Memoirists operate on a continuum between recollection and dramatization. Once one decides to re-create scenes, a line has been crossed and some invention necessarily follows. "Imaginative memoir" might be a good name for Conroy's book and the subgenre it represents. Even if most memoirs are not as fully imaginative as his, none that strive to dramatize moments in the past can be wholly faithful to knowable fact.

Clearly, the rules for reporting and remembering have to be different. For remembering, they simply have to be looser. How much looser depends on the writer and the writer's material. Some writers in some situations are strict constructionists. For example, Geoffrey Wolff in *The Duke of Deception*, an admirable, scrupulous, and extremely entertaining book. The book's two central characters are the author and his father, a confidence man, or, as Wolff calls him in the first chapter, "a bullshit artist." It must have been obvious to Wolff that some readers were going to wonder: *Like father, like son?* Factual accuracy is usually an implicit issue in nonfiction, but Wolff makes it explicit. *The Duke of Deception* is a reported memoir. Wolff interviewed other people, including his mother, and he makes those interviews part of his story, complicating and sometimes contradicting his own memory. He lets the reader see how he knows what he says he knows. He is also unusually restrained in his use of dialogue.

Many memoirists quote pages of talk that was uttered decades back, dialogue they can't possibly have remembered exactly. Memoirists do this so often as to leave a reader with only two options: to stop reading most memoirs, or to accept remembered dialogue as artistically licensed in this genre, as a convention of the form, like a papier-mâché sky at the back of a stage or the propensity of characters in an opera to break into song.

In her classic growing-up memoir, *Memories of a Catholic Girlhood*, Mary McCarthy talks about this very problem and sets out an unusually clear and thorough set of rules for writing engagingly in the present while being faithful to the past. "Quotation marks," she tells us, "indicate that a conversation to this general effect took place, but I do not vouch for the exact words or the exact order of the speeches." She reflects on the memoirist's dilemma, particularly if the memoirist happens also to be a novelist. "Many a time, in the course of doing these memoirs, I have wished that I were writing fiction. The temptation to invent has been very strong, particularly where recollection is hazy and I remember the substance of an event but not the details—the color of a dress, the pattern of a carpet, the placing of a picture." But she resisted.

A candid admission of the frailty of memory can certainly be overdone, but it can establish a bona fide with the reader, and perhaps achieve something more than that, by naming, at least, what cannot be re-created. Mary Karr, in her memoir *Lit*, describes a domestic quarrel in some detail, but then remarks that its aftermath, a reconciliation, is irretrievable: "If we talked about the night before, I don't recall it, which isn't fair to either of us, for it doesn't show our reasoned selves paring away at our scared ones. . . . The shrieking fight or the out-of-character insult endures forever, while the daily sweetness dissolves like sugar in water."

For some writers there comes a moment when the "truth" of experience seems not just out of reach but somehow at odds with the facts, or when the facts seem simply insufficient. Maybe that is the time to forsake memoir and write a novel. Something like this seems to have happened to one prominent memoirist, Tim O'Brien, but with the unusual result that the facts refused to be ignored.

Perhaps no contemporary has better demonstrated the tension between memory and memoir than O'Brien, most of whose writing life has been informed by the harrowing year he spent as an infantryman in Vietnam. Soon after the experience, in 1975, he published his memoir of the war, *If I Die in a Combat Zone.* Critics honored the book for its immediacy and its honesty. None expressed any doubt as to its authenticity, but it seems to have left O'Brien himself unsatisfied.

Years later he published *The Things They Carried*, which drew on the same experience but which he described as a "work of fiction." If you were an appreciative reader of the first book, then *The Things They Carried*, though equally if not more powerful, was oddly disconcerting. The book seemed to insist that *it*, not the memoir, was the true story of O'Brien's war. "I want you to feel what I felt," O'Brien writes. "I want you to know why story-truth is truer sometimes than happening-truth." This can be understood in a perfectly straightforward way: only by heightening reality could O'Brien communicate the true dimensions of his own emotions. But things get more convoluted than that. This is a "work of fiction" that insists on its own veracity. To start, O'Brien refers to himself by his own name, and as the book's dedication reveals, he also uses the real names of the men he served with. (Their names had been changed in his memoir.) And after more than one scene, he disowns what he has just written, stepping back to say: No, that wasn't the way it was. Here's the way it really was.

Take for instance the chapter "Speaking of Courage," which tells the story of a soldier named Norman Bowker. We see Bowker after the war has ended, aimless and assaulted by memories of his experience, lamenting his failure to save a dying comrade. The scene of the death is grotesque—a monsoon-soaked field that has been used as an outdoor toilet by the villagers nearby, "a field of shit." The wounded soldier drowns in the mud and excrement in the middle of the night. Bowker wants to talk to someone about what happened, but he trusts no one to understand. He imagines saying that he could have won the Silver Star had he saved his friend, but it becomes plain he is masking his guilt, and the story he really wants to tell is about the complicity he feels in the man's death. Taken as it stands, the piece would be a fully realized short story. It is soon obvious, however, that it is not meant to be taken as it stands, because O'Brien undercuts (and enlarges) it, in a subsequent piece called "Notes." He writes: ". . . I want to make it clear Norman Bowker was in no way responsible for what happened to [the dead soldier]. Norman did not experience a failure of nerve that night. He did not freeze up or lose the Silver Star for valor. That part of the story is my own." The author says, "It was hard stuff for me to write." And having been shown the ways in which the author has tried to avoid writing it, the reader is invited to feel the shame that he, Tim O'Brien—a living man, not confined to a printed page—presumably does feel.

Or maybe not. One could argue reasonably that if the book is fiction, then anything in it might be invented. The playwright has stepped onstage but he's still part of the play. We can presume to have no idea what he is really like. But at that level of contrivance the essential effort of the work would be dissipated; the reader wouldn't "feel what I felt." The device, not the emotion, would become the subject. The book as a whole resists such a reading. It seems to want to tell the truth about a real Tim O'Brien in a real war. We are left with the strange sense that the "work of fiction" is the true memoir, not true as to "feeling" alone, but also true as to fact. Or to the facts as O'Brien knows them.

•

The desire to tell the truth haunts the serious memoirist, and so it should. But there is a step beyond truth. For the writer, the ultimate reward of memoir may be to produce a work in which the facts are preserved but the experience is transformed.

In *A Fortunate Man*, a meditation on the working life of an English country doctor, John Berger writes: "Perhaps this is the true attraction of autobiography: all the events over which you had no control are at last subject to your decision." Writers in all genres are attracted to the promise of control over past events— if by "control" one means creating form or finding patterns in a life or a mind or the world, and, in the case of memoir, finding a road through the wilderness of one's past.

Some memories cry out for this kind of control, as in the case of a young man with a painful past who had a powerful story to tell, but was uncertain about whether to tell it. His name is Pacifique.* He grew up in an African country beset by civil war. His parents—farmers and herders—were virtually illiterate and yet they valued education, and Pacifique managed to attend grade school, often in peril from trigger-happy soldiers. He did well. His test scores were among the country's highest and earned him a secondary school education. Then, at nineteen, through a series of improbable accidents and charitable acts, he was brought

*Pacifique is a friend of both the authors'; he asks us to identify him by his first name alone.

to the United States, where he spent a year at the private secondary school Deerfield Academy.

English was still strange to him when he arrived. (He was fluent in French as well as in his native language.) He had never read a great novel or poem, but as a child he had conceived a fondness for the kinds of stories that elders had traditionally told—mixtures of fact and fiction that the elders always claimed were true, with complicated structures leading invariably to a moral.

A frequent lesson of the elders' stories was the importance of discretion. Pacifique came from a culture that values silence, and so by training he was disinclined to tell his new schoolmates much about his past. Moreover, he worried that American students and teachers would be afraid of him if they knew about the violence in which he had grown up. They might think that it had left him violent too. But as he learned more English, he began to set down some of his experiences. When his teacher told him that some of what he had written was "damn near publishable," Pacifique said he only wanted to improve his English. The very idea of making his stories public seemed to frighten him. He worried that his stories were unfit even for his teacher to read because they contained so much horror. His teacher tried to reassure him, telling him that art had the great power to transform the experience of suffering and injustice into something beautiful. This idea made a strong impression on Pacifique.

In one of the stories he wrote—he called it "The Color of a Sound"—Pacifique begins with a glass breaking in the dining hall at Deerfield. The sound triggers a memory. His native village is being attacked—on "one of the days my mother apologized to my brother and me for having given birth to us." The family's house is burned down. He and his mother and brother spend the night hiding in the forest. In the morning, standing near a clearing, Pacifique witnesses the killing of a young school-mate named Patrick. The boy has been tricked into approaching a rebel soldier. The soldier is holding a glass. The soldier drops it on purpose, and the glass shatters. Pacifique explains a super-stition in his country, that if you drop something you are eating or drinking, you may blame a person near you for wanting it. The soldier accuses Patrick of having wanted his drink, then orders him to pick up the shards of glass and put them in his mouth. The soldier forces Patrick to chew, then shoots him in the forehead. The story ends this way:

Because I had seen so many killings and would see ones even more horrifying, I thought I would forget Patrick's, but eleven years later, when I arrived at Deerfield Academy, Pat-rick returned. In the dining hall whenever I heard a glass shatter, I did not think of the superstition. I thought of Pat-rick's mouth full of glass and would see him trying to bite. My mouth would be full of food and I could not take a bite. It was as if the food in my mouth had become the pieces of glass.

When my fellow students heard a sound of a glass break-ing, they knew someone dropped a glass and they would laugh at that person's clumsiness. When I heard the sound of a glass breaking, I would not laugh. I would see a red color instead. The color of blood in Patrick's mouth. A color no one else could see.

During his first year in America, involuntary memories were an important problem for Pacifique—the dreadful things he could not banish from his mind, gusts of memory that could come at any time. Two years later, he felt that something important had changed. While writing, he said, he had discovered a partial defense against his memories: "That's how it started. I wrote a story and I felt relieved. I could control it. In the head, I could not. It's as if you had your hands on it and you could control it and make it beautiful. So instead of it having power on you, you had power on it. When it comes as a memory, it dictates to you, it controls you. After I wrote that story about the breaking glass, I would hear a glass breaking but it never came back that way. I mean, I would remember what happened, but it was never as before. I would think of making some modification in the story, to make the story better. Then if a memory woke me up, I could get back to sleep by writing it down, thinking I could turn it into something beautifully written. I mean, that's what I wish."

He didn't show his stories to other students. He still wasn't eager to make his past public, but he wasn't afraid of that anymore. He was afraid that other students would tell him the stories weren't well made, and because their command of English was superior to his, he would be obliged to believe them. Most writers are vulnerable to criticism. It is hard to imagine one more vulnerable than Pacifique. Writing had been a great discovery for him, a defense against the invasions of memory, a way to get to sleep. But when he wrote stories that included the horrors of his past, he had to believe that the stories were well made, or could be remade until they were. Otherwise, memory would regain its hold. "If it isn't well written," he said, "it is as if it comes back into you."

Many writers have spoken about memoir as a way to "objectify" experience, to get clarifying "distance" between oneself and one's past. But that was not precisely what Pacifique intended when he spoke of having power over his memories, nor is it the highest use of memoir. One can also use memoir to get *closer* to the past.

The memories that surface suddenly—merely unpleasant for most people, horrifying for Pacifique—are bolts from a bigger storm, capricious, even random. If you can go back to the source and see your memories whole, you can create truer versions of what you remember. You tell the stories as accurately and artfully as your abilities allow. If you succeed, you replace the fragments of memory with something that has its own shape and meaning, a separate thing that has value in itself. The past becomes an assertion that your life is of the present and the future.

Taking the undifferentiated materials left by the past and giving them pattern and form can be—more than solace—a source of great pleasure. The delight that memoir can offer is like the delight a woodworker may feel when putting the finishing touches on a beautiful desk. The desk is different from the wood forever. And the good memoir is different from the memories behind it, not a violation of them but different, and different of course from the actual experience that gave birth both to memory and to memoir.

4

ESSAYS

_____

I awoke one morning to discover that I was an essayist. It was not what I had in mind for myself, to be painfully frank. I had published a book, The Thing Itself: On the Search for Authenticity, *which I had imagined as—well, treatise is certainly too strong a word. Meditation? Maybe. But really I had simply thought of it as a book. Now I discovered that it was an essay. Actually, some reviewers said it was a series of essays. I had thought of these pieces as united by their theme, and indeed had written them that way. But the subjects ranged from antiques to climate change to television news to unicorns. I had to admit that they could be read independent of the order in which I had so deliberately put them.*

As an essayist friend of mine has pointed out, one of the problems with the essay, as a form, is that everyone has written one. You can easily make your way through life without writing a novel or a poem, but it is hard to get out of high school without writing an essay. It thus becomes an unexalted endeavor. And yet strangely enough the essay is an outsider's genre. Essays tend to be critical, subversive of something or other, even if it is just the latest fashion in sunglasses.

In the family of writers, essayists play poor cousins to writers of fic-

tion or narrative nonfiction. But great things have been accomplished in essays, which are the natural medium of ideas. Essays yield many of the nuggets of wisdom that inform everyday life, including the one line of Emerson's that everyone knows: "A foolish consistency is the hobgoblin of little minds." This observation, the schoolboy's friend, might also serve as a credo for the essayist. Essays are a congenial form for the divided mind. Once, years ago, I was teaching a course in English literature. By midsemester the students knew me quite well. One morning I was groping for a phrase, "And, and . . ." "And yet?" a voice said helpfully. Only then did I realize that "and yet" had become my signature idiom, emblem of the contradictions that I wanted the students to see on every hand. Emblem, too, of the contradictions within my own skull. Essayists tend to argue with themselves. The inner dialogue that might be suppressed in other writing finds a forum here. Montaigne blessed the form when he said, "If I knew my own mind, I would not make essays. I would make decisions."

—RT

There is something you want to say, and yet you are dogged by the perennial questions—sometimes useful, but sometimes fatal—that can visit any writer. Who am I to be writing this? Who asked me? And cruelest of all, Who cares?

When you write about your own ideas, you put yourself in a place that can feel less legitimate than the ground occupied by reporters or even by memoirists, who are, or ought to be, authorities on their subjects. An all-purpose term describes efforts at sharing your mind: the essay. As an essayist you can sometimes feel like a public speaker who must build his own stage and lectern. Essays are self-authorizing. This is the dilemma but also the pleasure of the form. The chances are that nobody asked for your opinion. But if your idea is fresh, it will surprise even someone, perhaps an assigning editor, who did ask.

Most good essays transcend argument. *Thoreau argues in favor of walking, says we need to spend more time in nature* might be the unhelpful gloss of the great essay "Walking." All its wide-ranging declarations live through the force of personal conviction. Most of the work that we call personal essay goes beyond logic and fact into the sovereign claims of idiosyncrasy. This is not to suggest that essays should be illogical, but they may be, and generally should be, *extra*-logical—governed by associative more than by strictly linear thought. Writers who are used to the strictures and scruples of journalism can find themselves stymied by the essay, inhibited by the freedom thrust upon them.

The great essayists of the past have in their various ways established the contemporary essayist's rights. Montaigne virtually invented the form. Emerson and Thoreau defined it for America, and never before or since has the essay had such cultural sway. *Walden,* though a full-length book, is essentially an essay, or even (in its loose confederation of ideas) a collection of essays. In a classroom today, Emerson and Thoreau may be remembered as otherworldly spirits who wrote in opposition to the materialism of their time. But on the page they were swashbucklers. Thoreau might have been our best-known hermit, but if you listen to him at the start of "Walking," it is not a hermit's reticence that you encounter:

I wish to speak a word for Nature, for absolute Freedom
and Wildness, as contrasted with a Freedom and Culture
merely civil—to regard man as an inhabitant, or a part and
parcel of Nature, rather than a member of society. I wish to
make an extreme statement, if so I may make an emphatic
one . . .

Thoreau revels in extravagance and hyperbole. One would
pay to hear the tone of voice in which he read his work aloud—as
he often did, despite his stylized reclusion. "Walking" debuted as
a lecture in 1851. It is laced with humor and self-mockery. It
seems likely that his stirring flights of eloquence were recog-
nized by his audience as pieces of showmanship, appreciated as
much for their theatricality as their content. Thoreau is gener-
ous with assertions. He goes on flights of imagery and specula-
tion:

The Hindoos dreamed that the earth rested on an elephant, and the elephant on a tortoise . . . It will not be out of
place here to state, that a fossil tortoise has lately been discovered in Asia large enough to support an elephant.

In an essay by Thoreau, the "I" is the measure of all things.
All its experience can be brought to bear; no subject is too small
to notice or too big to contemplate. Emerson wrote even more
expansively and aphoristically, and in describing the transcen-
dentalist he contributed the ultimate metaphor for the essayist's
relationship to the world: "I become a transparent eyeball."

•

What gives you license to write essays? Only the presence of an idea and the ability to make it your own. People speak of the "personal essay" as a form, but all essays are personal. They may make sweeping pronouncements, but they bear the stamp of an individual mind. Original ideas, those hinges on which an era turns, are rare. It is unlikely that you will write *The Origin of Species*. Or that you will be Emerson. But originality and profundity are not identical. Profound ideas bear repeating, or rediscovery, and many original ideas do not. Essays are like poems in that they may confront old wisdom in a fresh way. That Shakespeare wrote of the bittersweetness of parting did not preclude Emily Dickinson from doing so, too. Essays illustrate the truth that, just as no word has an exact synonym, no idea can be exactly paraphrased. Essays often gain their authority from a particular sensibility's fresh apprehension of generalized wisdom. But the point is not to brush aside the particular in favor of the general, not to make everything into a grand idea, but to treat something specific with such attention that it magnifies into significance. As Theodor Adorno says, ". . . the desire of the essay is not to seek and filter the eternal out of the transitory; it wants, rather, to make the transitory eternal."

For writers, the essay can offer an escape from the tyranny of Importance. You don't need to have fought wars, climbed mountains, received the confidences of presidents; you can have the most mundane of experiences and make something that surpasses them. Some essays prove that you are free in fact to make a great deal out of nothing. In Virginia Woolf's "Street Haunting," for example, the nominal subject is the writer's errand in the early evening, a stroll to a stationer's store in search of a pencil. The stroll becomes the occasion for thought about the nature of solitude, and about the consolidation of self in the home versus the dissolution of self in the city. The small experience keeps ramifying into something else. She remembers standing on the doorstep of the stationer's and thinks, "It is always an adventure to enter a new room, for the lives and characters of its owners have distilled their atmosphere into it, and directly we enter it we taste some new wave of emotion." The reader's eye adjusts to this level of magnification. It seems to be in the nature of essays that they invite us into digressions of thought all our own. Woolf's reader today, inured to chain stores, might reflect on what it used to be like when much of the mercantile world consisted of little shops like the one she describes, when entering a store meant stepping into someone else's world.

The essayist's relationship with the reader depends, as always, on mutual trust, but trust of a special kind. In the essay, trust in the author and disagreement with the author can coexist. In an essay about essays—"She: Portrait of the Essay as a Warm Body"—Cynthia Ozick describes her experience of reading Emerson:

I may not be persuaded by Emersonianism as an ideology, but Emerson—his voice, his language, his music—persuades me. . . . I may regard (or discard) the idea of the soul as no better than a puff of warm vapor. But here is Emerson on the soul: "When it breathes through [man's] intellect, it is genius; when it breathes through his will, it is virtue; when it flows through his affection, it is love." And then—well, I am in thrall; I am possessed; I believe.

You ask the reader to take *you* seriously, to honor your conviction even if your ideas provoke more than they persuade. You want engagement at least as much as you want belief. You welcome the silent dialogue with the reader, even if the reader is disputing with you. After all, you are often in dispute with yourself: beliefs are reached in the course of writing, and essays trace the course. "How do I know what I mean until I hear what I say?" is the familiar line. But its opposite is also true: How do I know what I *don't* mean until I hear what I say? Essays let you second-guess yourself, even contradict yourself in front of the reader. Self-doubt, fatal in so many enterprises, fortifies the essay.

•

All the genres blur, but none is blurrier than the essay, and it comes in so many varieties that attempts to delineate it are constantly thwarted. In America we think of the patriarchs Emerson and Thoreau and of their sure-handed assertions about Nature and Self-Reliance. A century and a half later we have John D'Agata's anthology *The Next American Essay*. It includes one piece written entirely in lowercase and without punctuation (David Antin's manifesto, "The Theory and Practice of Post-Modernism"). Another piece, Jenny Boully's "The Body," is a bodiless text consisting entirely of footnotes to blank pages.

The line between essay and memoir is particularly porous.

You may turn to the essay as a refuge from memoir, and essays may then serve as covert memoirs: you say some things about yourself, while you generalize from your experience in ways that seem worth the reader's attention. George Orwell's "Such, Such Were the Joys" appears in his collected essays, but for most of the way it reads as a memoir of his desperate schoolboy days at the British boarding school that he calls Crossgates. Most readers would be entranced by Orwell's account of the parsimonious suppers, the cold baths, the canings. But something in the essayist wants to make statements. Orwell broadens the piece into wisdom about the nature of childhood itself, with a direct appeal to the reader's own experience (universally different, in the present day, from Orwell's): "Look back into your own childhood and think of the nonsense you used to believe and the trivialities which could make you suffer." There is something uplifting about this stance, which takes the essay beyond the uniqueness of personal experience, beyond "poor me." Orwell offers this refreshing view on the vagaries of memory: "But it can also happen that one's memories grow sharper after a long lapse of time, because one is looking at the past with fresh eyes and can isolate and, as it were, notice facts which previously existed undifferentiated among a mass of others." In this way, an essayist may make a subtle but fiercer claim for himself than can the memoirist. Orwell is not claiming to re-create the past but to understand what he remembers best. He doesn't lament the evanescence of memory. What's gone is gone, what's left behind is better. Good riddance to the stinging of the buttocks or the gnawing in the stomach. What remains is a greater lucidity in the mind.

"Historicize yourself," the essayist Christopher Cokinos advises would-be writers of memoir. He means that they should turn their memoirs into essays. In his view, conventional memoir can become a self-created prison, but the essay can illuminate both the public and the private by placing the self in the context of time, politics, ideas. A term for this mode of writing has sprung up: the "braided essay." It relies on what is meant to be artful juxtaposition. In "Castro's Beard," Jeff Porter interweaves his boyhood with Cold War events that were happening simultaneously but outside his consciousness. An account of the Soviet ships approaching Cuba with a complement of missiles is followed without transition by a paragraph taking us to a Little League game: "In the top of the third inning I am hit by a pitch."

In much of her work, Joan Didion uses the first person as a tuning fork, to pick up the vibrations of an age. Her essay "The White Album" is redolent of the social confusion of the 1960s, and a perfect example of the first person as an authenticator of experience. One passage begins with a psychiatric report: "a personality in process of deterioration with abundant signs of failing defenses and increasing inability of the ego to mediate the world of reality and to cope with normal stress." Didion breaks into the report to say: "The patient to whom this report refers is me." She goes on to acknowledge that she has been suffering from vertigo and nausea, and then says, "By way of comment I offer only that an attack of vertigo and nausea does not now seem to me an inappropriate response to the summer of 1968." And off she goes, to all sorts of what have become file-footage legends—the depredations of the "Manson family," the rise and fall of the Black Panthers, the drug-addled music scene in Los Angeles. Didion's best-known sentence, "We tell ourselves stories in order to live," begins this essay, and the theme is the inverse of that sentence. She is telling us that the narrator cannot make sense of the madness around her.

"The White Album" is another example of an essay that might be read as memoir. But the author isn't seeking self-understanding, nor does the reader wish exactly to understand her. Instead, she uses her own responses to the times as a means of trying to capture a broad truth about events. In her own mild and stylized derangement, she might be accused of participating in the mimetic fallacy: to describe chaos, write chaotically. But the chaos isn't in the writing itself, which is dramatic but measured and precise. The sense of chaos comes from her using the self as an embodiment of its surroundings. The argument for this device is simply that it accomplishes its purpose; for people who were sentient back then, it brings back the febrile state of the culture. The argument against such prose is that it enacts not egotism but egocentrism, the placing of oneself at the center of the universe.

But that follows in the great tradition of essay writing. In the essay, one steps forward. Even in the rare case where the first person doesn't appear, an individual authority is summoned, as in the magisterial critical essays of T. S. Eliot. The self as the measure of all things has its moral hazards, but the essayist needs at least a dash of Emersonian confidence, and more than a dash is useful to some.

The essayist can also appear as a figure who boasts of little in the way of heightened emotion or peculiarity of feeling. This sort of writer's whole claim on the reader is the claim of the norm: *I am but a distillation of you.*

E. B. White achieves such a presence. His essays, though rooted in midcentury America, travel well through time. His enduring love letter to New York was published just after the Second World War, when an awareness of the power of the atomic bomb had changed perceptions of just about everything. The essay, "Here Is New York," for most of its length evokes the city's charm. Toward the end that quality is named, and given a new and sinister meaning, prophetic in the aftermath of the airborne attack on the World Trade Center:

> The city, for the first time in its long history, is destructible. A single flight of planes no bigger than a wedge of geese can quickly end this island fantasy . . . All dwellers in cities must live with the stubborn fact of annihilation; in New York the fact is somewhat more concentrated because of the concentration of the city itself, and because, of all targets, New York has a certain clear priority. In the mind of whatever perverted dreamer might loose the lightning, New York must hold a steady, irresistible charm.

White and Didion may represent extremes, each admirable, in the essayist's use of the self. Atul Gawande offers an equally admirable example of the use of the professional self. Gawande is a surgeon and professor of medicine at Harvard, and he has published several books of essays on medical subjects. In "The Bell Curve," he contemplates a simple fact that most doctors find hard to discuss: that some of them are better than others. Gawande reports that the differences have become quantifiable and can be expressed in a bell curve, and he ponders the effects on patients and doctors alike. Though it is plain that Gawande writes with an implicit authority (and no doubt with special access) because of his professional identity, he never pulls rank on the reader. When he invokes his professional status it is to wonder how he would treat the news if he himself failed to measure up to the profession's highest standards:

> If we . . . discovered that I am one of the worst, the answer would be easy: I'd turn in my scalpel. But what if I were a B–? Working as I do in a city that's mobbed with surgeons, how could I justify putting patients under the knife? I could tell myself, Someone's got to be average. If the bell curve is a fact, then so is the reality that most doctors are going to be average. There is no shame in being one of them, right?
>
> Except, of course, there is.

"The Bell Curve" is of general worth for the issue it raises, and it also has great value for a writer of essays. In discovering the right place to stand in relation to his subject, Gawande accomplishes what every writer must accomplish. In his case, this means that, without removing his white coat, he becomes something more than a "professional." An essay both allows and requires you to say something more than you are entitled to say by virtue of your résumé alone.

In one of its modes—humor—the essay sometimes breaks the basic rule of nonfiction. Wit can confer the freedom to fictionalize. Ian Frazier has written distinguished reportage, but he is also a gifted social satirist. In "Thanks for the Memory," for instance, he assumes the role of Bob Hope, in a parody of the co-median's vacuous public utterances, recalling a golf tournament: "The payoff was over half a billion dollars, just for me. It's one of the largest amounts of money there is."

The humorous essay often turns on self-mockery, and once you are mocking yourself, the reader is less likely to dispute your right to use hyperbole. David Sedaris, the best-known cur-rent master of the humorous essay, came to literary prominence with his "SantaLand Diaries," an essay that describes his service as one of Santa's elves at Macy's department store in New York. This piece skewers not only a commercialized Christmas holiday but the overbearing mothers and insufferable children who cel-ebrate it. Does Sedaris overstate when he says that he told a misbehaving child that Santa would come to his house and steal his television and all his appliances? Doubtless so, but the piece rests on the absurdity of its author's role, the basic facts of which we understand to be true. It's a subtle balance; the piece would not be so funny if he were "making the whole thing up." You need to know that real pain was involved. It takes some courage to admit to having been a hired elf. Having done so, you may be forgiven a scene like the one in which Sedaris claims to have used sign language as he said to a deaf child in a loud clear voice: "SANTA HAS A TUMOR IN HIS HEAD THE SIZE OF AN OLIVE. MAYBE IT WILL GO AWAY TOMORROW BUT I DON'T THINK SO."

•

What can you learn from practitioners of the essay, in all its variety? There can't be many general lessons for a form that depends so heavily on nerve and poise and on having something idiosyncratic to say. Every essayist deals with the same general ingredients—self and experience and idea—but everyone deals with them differently. Good essayists share the ability and the confidence to use the power of their own highly specified convictions.

Edward Hoagland, although he has worked in other forms, is nonetheless known primarily for his essays. Writing in the 1970s, in a turbulent political season, Hoagland begins "Of Cows and Cambodia" by allying himself with the big stories of the hour:

> During the invasion of Cambodia, an event which may rate little space when recent American initiatives are summarized but which for many of us seemed the last straw at the time, I made an escape to the woods. The old saw we've tried to live by for an egalitarian half-century that "nothing human is alien" has become so pervasive a truth that I was worn to a frazzle. I was the massacre victim, the massacring soldier, and all the gaudy queens and freaked-out hipsters on the street.

No one gives you permission to write this way. It is like taking a bite of the apple that is the world. You do it. You get away with it. Soon experience entitles you to do it again.

5

BEYOND ACCURACY

===============

Fact

Some authors admit to having altered facts in narratives that are described as nonfiction. In an endnote to *About a Mountain*, John D'Agata writes:

> Although the narrative of this essay suggests that it takes place over a single summer, the span between my arrival in Las Vegas and my final departure was, in fact, much longer. I have conflated time in this way for dramatic effect only, but I have tried to indicate each instance of this below. At times, I have also changed subjects' names or combined a number of subjects into a single composite "character." Each example of this is noted.

What has just happened here? We have come to the end of a nonfiction story and now the author tells us that we can rely on the accuracy of almost nothing we have just read. This might be called a literary experiment, and no one wants to condemn experiments out of hand. But writers might consider what they give up when they abandon fact.

Sometimes legal and moral constraints force a nonfiction storyteller to change a character's name or in other ways disguise a character's identity. Most readers will accept such changes, especially if the author announces them at the start. Not intending to change anything, scrupulous reporters get facts wrong sometimes. These departures from fact are different in kind from deliberate alterations that are made for the author's convenience—for instance, to enhance a story's clarity or drama. A literary critic would have reason for asking, Is this writer just taking an easy way around the disappointments of reality? To engage the world through what is knowable; to express with clarity the drama and indeed the truth that may be lurking in the facts, within actual and not composite individuals, within real and not fictional events; to find a good story and tell it well *while* sticking to the facts—for many writers of factual narratives, those are the basic challenges and opportunities of the form. Defining "nonfictional" time in this spirit does not mean that one must always tell the events of a story in the order in which they happened or never assemble events drawn from disparate times. What it does mean is not substituting made-up dates for real ones.

One large risk of fictionalizing is a loss of faith by both writer and reader. When writers stop believing in their own stories, readers tend to sense it. You the writer might solve your own problem by telling the reader after the fact, "Things didn't happen quite the way I said, but wouldn't it be nice if they had." But such an admission may well leave the reader feeling cheated. Surely most readers come to a piece of writing that is called nonfiction with a reasonable expectation that the writer will at the very least attempt to be faithful to knowable facts. If you violate that expectation, you create a different set of expectations. If you abandon the goal of accuracy, you take on not just the freedoms but also the obligations of fiction. You ask that your entire story be judged by fiction's standards. John McPhee once put the matter in an opposite way: "Things that are cheap and tawdry in fiction work beautifully in nonfiction because they are true. That's why you should be careful not to abridge it, because it's the fundamental power you're dealing with. You arrange it and present it. There's lots of artistry. But you don't make it up."

Assume, if only for the sake of argument, that accuracy as to facts is a worthy goal for writers of nonfiction narratives. It is not a trivial undertaking. If you think about the matter, it's clear that complete accuracy is unattainable. Every story has a history, and the actors and witnesses will all remember it differently—that is, if they're still alive and willing to talk and haven't colluded in concocting a sanitized version. As for events that you witnessed yourself, your perceptions may be easier to sort out, but they, too, are bound to be incomplete.

The impossible but useful goal of trying to notice everything does not of course imply the goal of recording everything. In a job of long-term reporting—listening to the same people day after day, month after month—synoptic notes and voice recordings would leave you with something like the map that Jorge Luis Borges imagines: a map of the world that is perfectly accurate and as big as the world.

But you do your best. To reconstruct a story, you chase after accuracy—checking one subject's memories against another's, looking for the trail of records that you know exists somewhere.

And when you witness a story or part of one, you record your perceptions as honestly and precisely as you can.

BEYOND FACT

A parable.

When I was a boy, children were regarded differently. A lot of the time we were not regarded much at all. We were incidental to adult life. I'm sure they loved us, though of course they didn't say so. The word "love" generally was reserved in those days for music on the radio. The upside of this was that we children were allowed to see a lot, especially if we shut up. For instance, perfectly respectable people would not think anything of taking a child into a bar. Thus it was that I found myself more than once perched on a stool next to my grandfather when I was four or five years old, having ginger ale as he had what he called a "snort or two." The bar in my mind's eye had an elk's head mounted on the wall. I may have asked my grandfather how the elk's head came to be there, or maybe he simply took it upon himself to tell me the story. It was quite sad, he said. One day the poor elk had come crashing through the wall, and they had just left him there. "The rest of him is sticking out the back," he said. "We'll go around and look at him someday."

To me, this little story expresses the difference between fiction and nonfiction, and not in the sense you might think, that my grandfather was a liar. Imagine that the bar is a book. In a novel, the mounted elk's head is all there is. But in nonfiction, the rest of the elk really is on the other side of the wall.

—RT

Nonfiction writers portray actual events and actual people. But no matter how faithful to the facts, what you write can never be co-extensive with what you are writing about. Of necessity things get left out. One might say that the fiction writer leaves things out, too. But while the reader imagines things left unsaid, the fact is that if they aren't in the novel, they don't exist. It is an agreeable fantasy, when you come to the end of a novel, to wonder what happened next to the characters. But you know that nothing happened next. The book ends, and the characters end with it. They may live forever in the imagination, but they have no lives outside the novel. In nonfiction characters do have lives. Usually, those lives do go on after the book ends. Those people have lives that were in place before they became "characters." They have actions and meanings and emotions that inevitably lie outside what a piece of writing can describe.

All this is obvious. And yet writers of fact forget it at their peril. It is one important source of the moral complexity at the heart of the enterprise of nonfiction.

One still encounters some people in journalism—in some newsrooms or maybe at the Fox network—who talk of objectivity. They are more or less harmless. Either they are disingenuous or they are dunces, and in either case they pose little threat. We know that as soon as writers begin to tell a story they shape experience and that stories are always, at best, partial versions of reality, and thus objectivity is a myth. More worrisome are people who want to pursue the other line of argument, that "everything is subjective." Well, of course, everything is subjective, once you get beyond the very barest of facts. Imagine an immutable fact, a corpse lying on the floor, with a visible wound to the head. But the moment you call that corpse a victim, you begin to tell a story, and if you enlarge that to "victim of a senseless crime," then you have the makings of a plot. So yes, of course, just about everything is subjective. But people who take a particular glee in that idea usually have other agendas. It is only a couple of steps to the idea that all opinions are equally valuable, that because truth is multifaceted, and indeed infinite if you slice it finely enough, then all truth is equally valuable and equally suspect. "If it's true for you, then it's true"—that whole quagmire of postmodern nihilism. Subjectivity is for some people a disinhibiting drug. It absolves them of responsibility.

But subjectivity properly understood is really just another name for thought. Subjectivity simply acknowledges the presence of a mediator between the facts and the truth. That mediator is you, the writer. Acknowledging subjectivity absolves you of nothing. On the contrary, it makes you the one who has to explore the facts, discover what you can of the truth, and find the way to express that truth in prose—knowing as you look for the way to do this that you cannot be complete, that every inclusion implies countless exclusions, that you must strive to do no violence to those facts and those truths that compete for your attention.

The better a writer is at creating a portrait of someone, the more hazardous the process becomes. If you were writing a feature story for the Saturday edition of a newspaper and you quoted someone saying something mildly embarrassing, readers would know that you had not given them the whole person. But if you devote a book or a detailed and subtle magazine piece to portraying a human being, you are hoping that the reader will read with full imagination and that each detail you mention will resonate in a way that suggests things not actually written. The better you do this, the more the reader is apt to forget that the character has another life. And the truth is, you half want the reader to forget. You strive to give the reader the illusion of a real person, and you have to make sure that the illusion is faithful to the truth as you understand it.

To do this can lead you into peculiar situations, situations that may even put you at odds with some of the facts. It is obvious that the facts are always more numerous than can be accommodated, and that you have to select among them. Moreover, you have to remember that writing and reading are different from experience, and that the mind has an ability to absorb and to order, simultaneously to see and not to see, and that this is an ability that prose strives in vain to imitate. The mind can accommodate contradictions that a story can't. Sometimes the only route to truth—to reproducing your sense of the true nature of the events you witnessed—is a detour around a part of the story that distorts the whole.

•

At the center of Kidder's Among Schoolchildren *is the teacher, Christine Zajac. A real person, her real name. Dispatches from Kidder suggested that the reporting for this project was not always compellingly interesting. Days could go by without anything dramatic happening. It was a story without news. But it was a story, whose layers of meaning accreted slowly and quietly. Then, one day, something happened that actually was dramatic and seemed at the moment certain to be included in the book. Basically, Mrs. Zajac, a skilled classroom* manager and a very likable figure, briefly lost it. The mother of one of the very troubled students in the class had once again failed to show up for an appointment. Mrs. Zajac mentioned this fact to the student, and she did so in front of the class. Afterward, she was properly aghast at herself. If you had been there, it's the thing you would have talked about that night and maybe for a couple of days afterward. And of course Kidder wrote the scene. But as the book took shape, the scene increasingly didn't fit. If you had been in the room you would have placed the teacher's indiscretion in the context of the whole year. But in the book it seemed disproportionately significant. It could be explained, managed for the reader, but no explanation could replicate that mental process by which we simultaneously register and dismiss anomalous information. And there's a good reason for this: the reader is, however dimly, aware that the author is making choices and feels that if some-thing is there, it is there for a reason. No matter how this scene was placed, it loomed too large—again, the difference between writing and experience. We sometimes think, "If only I could get it all down." But if you could get it all down, the all would be at once too much and not enough. Finally it occurred to us to ask, "Do we really need this scene at all?" And out it went, without regret.

But this was not the end of the story. Kidder's reporting yielded an oppressive wealth of notes, what seemed like a verbatim record of 178 days in that classroom. And the first draft for the book stood at twelve hundred manuscript pages. Two-thirds of it went away. But one scene got larger. It was a moment that was buried in the manuscript and only on reconsideration seemed to resonate with meaning. In the end it became a pivotal moment. It occurs in a section called "The Science Fair," describing an annual event at which the school's classes came together and students displayed projects they had made to illustrate *one or another scientific principle. Originally it was tempting to play this scene for comic relief, and there was plenty of comedy. For instance, the team of girls whose project was "food," for which they displayed "a box of oatmeal, a hamburger bun, a piece of white bread, a carton of milk, two potatoes, and a remnant of iceberg lettuce going brown." The whole section was at one point a candidate for cutting. But one episode kept nagging. A recalcitrant boy named Robert, a yearlong discipline problem, was truant from the Science Fair. Mrs. Zajac stormed off to find him. What she found brought her up short, and the moment became one in which she had to face her own shortcomings as a teacher and the odds that some of her students were up against:*

She looked at his desk, and then the tightness left her jaw. She let her shoulders sag, and her face turned as red as Robert's.

On Robert's desk she saw a weathered scrap of two-by-six with raggedly cut ends. On each of its longer edges was a flashlight battery, precariously secured to the board by a profusion of bent and twisted nails. A tangle of wires, twisted around other nails, covered the surface of the board. An attempt had been made to tape the ends of the wires to the batteries and to a small light bulb. The bulb had a broken filament. A hammer and some outsize nails lay on Robert's desk next to his project. He had tried to make an electric light. It suddenly looked like a very difficult thing to do.

Chris looked at the project and she saw all at once a Robert slightly different from the one she thought she'd known just a minute ago. All year long she had tried to get Robert to take a chance and make an effort. Now he had. He had tried and he had *sincerely* failed. And she had rewarded him with humiliation.

This is highly managed experience. The facts are slight: the pathetic project, the redness of the faces, the body language. Many of the facts are emotional and internal. They come, of course, not from the imagination but from interviews after the fact with the teacher.

So we have an account of reality that leaves out what at first seemed a salient event of the year, leaves it out altogether. And we have instead a minute description of an episode that most of us would have politely looked away from and promptly forgotten. It's interesting to note in passing that the first episode, the indiscreet remark, would have been irresistible to the camera, while the second would have been very difficult to film, at least in a documentary format. And it would have been hard to describe in conversation. But I think it proved the right event for the written word.

Facts and truth: not only are they not synonymous, but they often have a very tangential relationship. Although the truth must always be found in facts, some facts, sometimes, obscure the truth. Sometimes that essential effort of writing, making some things small and others big, includes making something invisible.

—RT

The world for the nonfiction writer is not a kit full of endlessly interesting parts waiting to be assembled, a garden of flowers waiting to be picked and arranged. If that were the case, life would still be complicated, but of course it isn't the case. The writer is part of the world, engages the world, affects and is affected by it. More specifically, nonfiction writers enter into a relationship of some kind with the people they are writing about—or, in the case of memoirists, they already have entered into such relationships, and now want to make use of them for purposes that may not suit everyone involved.

Journalists are asked how their presence has affected the behavior of the people they followed around. The question sounds reasonable, even important, but it can't be answered fully. No one can capture the ever-changing interaction between a writer and a subject: observing another person and describing one's observations, and being altered oneself in the process and thus altering the observations. Some writers seem to feel they can cut through this maze by writing in the first person and describing how they conducted their research, but the very terms of the problem make it insoluble. It's doubtful the problem can even be fully expressed.

It can be confronted, though. Some journalists begin talking to subjects without a notebook or voice recorder and ease into the role of reporter. Others think it's more honest to open their notebooks at once and keep them open. One aim is to get subjects used to this odd presence, the fact of a reporter in their lives. Custom, just being around a lot, can help bring a subject back to acting naturally.

You are a guest in your subject's life and ought to behave as a good guest would. Avoid extremes of behavior: talking all the time or not talking at all. Sometimes you may want to challenge or nettle your subject. But you don't want to supply the subject with thoughts of your own. To a third party looking in on the scene, it might appear that the reporter is duping a subject into setting wariness aside, into talking too much. But most adults who let a reporter into their lives understand the reporter's role. Most subjects expect, indeed most want, the reporter to stand back and let them talk.

The real problem begins when you start to write. To try to depict real people is to grant yourself an immense power over individual lives, and the power is easily abused. Again, consider the difference between facts and truth. You can string together a number of facts about someone and create a picture. It may be critical, it may be flattering. That picture may accord with your own best sense of who that person really is, but it may violate the subject's own sense of his or her identity. What rules govern this delicate process?

There are legal constraints. In the United States, a different standard applies to characters who are public as opposed to private figures. The distinction is an accepted principle of libel law. It is in fact very hard for a public figure to sue successfully for libel. The plaintiff has to prove that the defendant, in making the disputed statement, acted with "malice"—that is, with knowledge that the statement was false or with what the courts have called "reckless disregard for truth or falsity." Of course good writers want to do better than to stay within the limits of the law, but the point is that the famous get treated differently from the nonfamous.

Readers do not expect a journalist to provide a richly human, sympathetic compassion for the inner fears and demons of, say, a former vice president. It would be interesting and valuable and great, but no one demands it. Pretty much any information you can get, as long as it's true, is fair game with vice presidents. But there is a kind of writing whose very virtue is that it follows those who are not usually followed. It illuminates society by looking away from celebrities and turning to subjects who would not otherwise be known to the reader. In such cases, the standards are more exacting, legally and morally too.

Janet Malcolm, in *The Journalist and the Murderer*, has written what many consider the landmark book on the relations between writers and subjects. This is a book journalists love to hate. It features an extraordinary and memorable first paragraph*— especially memorable because it appeared in *The New Yorker*, the magazine that has published more distinguished journalism than any other magazine in history. Here was an assertion that the whole enterprise was rotten to the core:

> Every journalist who is not too stupid or too full of himself to notice what is going on knows that what he does is morally indefensible. He is a kind of confidence man, preying on people's vanity, ignorance, or loneliness, gaining their trust and betraying them without remorse. Like the credulous widow who wakes up one day to find the charming young man and all her savings gone, so the consenting subject of a piece of nonfiction writing learns—when the book or article appears—*his* hard lesson. Journalists justify their treachery in various ways according to their temperaments.

*I read the first paragraph and flung the magazine across the room, and picked it up again about twenty years later. —TK

The more pompous talk about freedom of speech and "the public's right to know"; the least talented talk about Art; the seemliest murmur about earning a living.

This passage introduces the story of a lawsuit. The defendant was the writer Joe McGinniss, the plaintiff a convicted murderer named Jeffrey MacDonald. He and McGinniss had made a deal before his trial: he would give McGinniss special access to his life and to his defense team at the trial; in return he'd receive some of the proceeds from the book. Plainly, he expected McGinniss to portray him as innocent, and in the beginning McGinniss intended to do so. The two men became friends, but by the end of the trial McGinniss had changed his mind. He came to believe that the man had in fact murdered his family. But he didn't tell his subject this. Indeed, he wrote him letters of sympathy even as he created in his manuscript the portrait of a monster. The letters are painfully embarrassing to read, and the murderer's lawyer used them to powerful effect, as does Malcolm. In the end, the suit was more or less successful; McGinniss agreed to pay MacDonald $325,000.

This story could not be more perfect for Malcolm's uses. Indeed the first criticism of her argument is the very perfection of the story it relies on. Hard cases make bad law, the lawyers say, and this is a difficult case, not the sort of case from which to draw sweeping generalizations about journalists and their subjects. And Malcolm makes no real attempt to see McGinniss's side; her excuse, the lamest in the journalist's arsenal, is that McGinniss wouldn't talk to her. But whatever one makes of the merits of the lawsuit, Malcolm's analysis has value—especially for journalists who wish that the matters she deals with had been left submerged.

Few journalists would condone lying in their private lives. And yet many nonfiction writers venerate *In Cold Blood*, for which Truman Capote appears to have lied shamelessly to his subjects. Maybe the moral standing of the person matters. Is it okay to lie to a killer but not to, say, a Rotarian? Most writers feel uncomfortable at best with Capote's methods, and condemn them even if they celebrate the book. And what about less dramatic cases? What about those little gray areas? How much candor is a subject owed? If for example your subject makes a racist remark, which you would in ordinary conversation object to, do you let it slide by? Probably you do. Do you laugh at the unfunny joke? Nothing wrong with that, surely. Do you smile noncommittally when you hear an opinion you disagree with? If asked outright whether you agree with your subject when you could not in fact disagree more, do you give a little murmur that could be interpreted as assent? Perhaps you say, "I see your point."

Malcolm argues that something dishonest tends to lurk in all relationships between authors and their subjects. Certainly, all such relationships contain competing narratives. The subject has a story, the writer has a story, and the two don't coincide exactly. They may diverge radically. Writer and subject each want something from the other. So what? Life is full of people with varied interests striking a deal. But a special moral hazard arises in the journalistic case, in the multiple opportunities for deception and in the imbalance of power. The relationship between subject and author, according to Malcolm, often amounts to a mutual seduction, in which the journalist inevitably occupies the stronger position: "The moral ambiguity of journalism lies not in its texts but in the relationships out of which they arise—relationships that are invariably and inescapably lopsided." You and your subject might, for instance, spend some of your time together trading stories about your lives, and you might let yourself imagine that this was a symmetrical part of your relationship, but only if you forget that your subject isn't writing down *your* stories.

Malcolm makes another point that is instructive and cautionary for writers: "The metaphor of the love affair applies to both sides of the journalist-subject equation, and the journalist is no less susceptible than the subject to its pleasures and excitements." (She goes on to talk about how Joe McGinniss's lawyer tried to point out that this part of him, the friend part, was sincere in his dealings with MacDonald, even as the writer part went about his work, and Malcolm grudgingly admits that this is not as crazy as it sounds.) Malcolm continues: "An abyss lies between the journalist's experience of being out in the world talking to people and his experience of being alone in a room writing."

She might have gone on about this "abyss." Surely anyone who has done a long stint of reporting recognizes the truth of the concept. One can sometimes feel a peculiar closeness to a subject, a compound of gratitude and sympathy, something that feels like true affection. And yet when the subject must in fact *become* a subject, must turn into words, that feeling changes. You the writer do not feel the same things you felt as interviewer and observer. And who is to know on which side of the abyss lies the true sentiment? But every journalist knows, and every reader has a right to expect, that what gets expressed in print usually comes from the clear-eyed, not to say cold-hearted, writer serving the needs of the story.

Some potential subjects seem to understand that they have more than one motive for letting a writer into their lives. Here is an actual e-mail from a potential subject to a writer:

> I suppose if I am honest one prominent reason I'd enjoy doing this has to do with my respect for you as a writer, and the narcissistic pleasure I imagine I would take in having my portrait drawn. This is probably naïve. Inevitably, if the portrait is true, there will be features that make me uncomfortable. Equally important, I hope, is the value in having people get a more intimate, detailed picture of what it is like to [perform my job].

This degree of prior understanding is rare. However, journalists can help subjects think through the implications of letting writers into their lives. The essential precaution is clarity about the nature of the arrangements. Here are some steps one might consider taking: Assume that all potential subjects don't understand what they might be getting into, and tell them what you know about the possible consequences, especially the unpleasant ones. Explain to subjects that there is no predicting how you will portray them or how they will feel about their portraits, or how readers will judge them, and that they can't determine any of this because you cannot give them control over what you write. If they want to keep certain areas private, they must name them before your research begins in earnest. Most subjects insist on boundaries. If you feel theirs are too restrictive, it's probably better to withdraw than to argue your way to a grudging agreement that might well be taken back a year later. You should also explain that many people find it hard to be scrutinized, and that for the subject, reading your book may be like gazing into a fun-house mirror.

You might want to phrase this admission more delicately, or recite it over a beer. But it is best to be forthright, and sometimes even forbidding, at the start of a project, when you have nothing to lose except what you think might make for a good story. And it's wise to have evidence that you have been at least forthright, perhaps in an exchange of letters or e-mails, or in a recording (being sure that it includes the fact that subjects know they're being recorded).

Such measures can erode the natural sympathy you hope to engender, but they can also prevent the sort of misunderstanding that, well short of a lawsuit, can be devastating to your project. And, most important, these warnings can serve as an acknowledgment that you are something more and less than a friend.

Sometimes subjects actually turn into friends. (And in the case of memoir, friends can turn into subjects, which can be even trickier.) If you feel a true emotional concern about your subjects during your research, do you then intervene in their lives? Adrian Nicole LeBlanc faced this question during the ten years she spent working on *Random Family*, a book that depends utterly on the author's evident sympathy for her subjects. She sometimes helped out the women she was writing about, by giving them small cash advances, by babysitting for them, by driving them to the hospital or jail. She was criticized for this, but in the special circumstances of her research, these acts seem only humane and a long way from so-called checkbook journalism, from paying subjects for their stories.

LeBlanc still occasionally sees the people she wrote about. They tell her she's not as much fun as she used to be. That is because now she really is a friend, treating them as a friend would—speaking up when she thinks they're doing something foolish, whereas before she felt constrained to remain an observer.

Janet Malcolm's jeremiad can't be dismissed. It is, however, willfully oblivious to the many good things that can happen between writer and subject, good things that can far outweigh misunderstandings and wounded feelings. And the Malcolm worldview seems to discount the great work that can be produced.

•

Even outside the pages of crime fiction, reporters are prone to cynicism of the universal-prejudice variety: the worst that can be thought about another human being must be true, simply because it is the worst. This is a quick way to feel smart—to see beneath the surfaces of things without even having to look. But of course cynicism limits, a priori, what can be discovered about other human beings. The truly cynical reporter never knows the pleasure, or relief, of submerging the self to try to understand another self, serving the self by escaping the self.

The source of what we love about a monumental writer like Chaucer is the breadth of his disposition toward humanity. This is the great thing about *The Canterbury Tales*, that there is room in Chaucer's philosophy for all his characters, from the bawdy Wife of Bath to the hypocritical Pardoner. Chaucerian room is a breadth of imagination. It isn't guaranteed by a breadth of experience, which can just as easily narrow as enlarge one's general view of other human beings. Successful imagination does not imply an endorsement of stupidity, viciousness, and evil, or an abandonment of judgment. A reporter should go out into the world armed with skepticism and disposed to question press releases. And there's nothing wrong with carrying hypotheses and expectations about what you're going to find, so long as you also bring along what Ron Suskind calls "the willingness to be surprised." This isn't very hard to cultivate, once you discover— a constant in reporting—that your preconceptions were wrong. Finding this out can be bracing. It can feel as if you're making real discoveries when you first, or once again, discover that the world is too complex to be imagined fully, that it needs to be watched.

There is another, essentially spiritual concern for nonfiction writers. It has to do not so much with loyalty to one's truth or to one's subjects' truth as with loyalty to oneself. George Orwell defines the subject in his essay "Why I Write." He begins to answer the question by relating a number of influences that writers can easily relate to—he was a bookish child, loved stories, and so on. Then he makes a surprising turn with the following passage:

Every line of serious work that I have written since 1936 has been written, directly or indirectly, *against* totalitarianism and *for* democratic Socialism, as I understand it. It

seems to me nonsense, in a period like our own, to think that
one can avoid writing of such subjects. Everyone writes of
them in one guise or another. It is simply a question of which
side one takes and what approach one follows. And the more
one is conscious of one's political bias, the more chance one
has of acting politically without sacrificing one's aesthetic
and intellectual integrity.

What I have most wanted to do throughout the past ten
years is make political writing into an art.

This passage, written in 1946, only one lifetime ago, seems
unnatural to some contemporary ears. The passage can make
one dream of an age when there was one cause in the Western
world to which all could be subsumed. At the same time, one
resists Orwell's sentiment. This is a reflexive reaction perhaps,
because for the whole of most current literary lives no language
has been more suspect than the language of political assertion.
And much of this suspicion is owed to George Orwell himself,
well known for having described the violence that politics can do
to the English language.

Most contemporary writers, most of the time, have lived, as
writers, by a code very different from the code of political engagement. They have sought truth outside the world of public
affairs. This is a code nicely expressed by Mark Kramer in his
introduction to the anthology *Literary Journalism:*

Literary journalism couples cold fact and personal event,
in the author's humane company. And that broadens readers'

scans, allows them to behold others' lives, often set within far clearer context than we can bring to our own. The process moves readers, and writers, toward realization, compassion, and in the best of cases, wisdom.

I'll even claim that there is something intrinsically political—and strongly democratic—about literary journalism, something pluralistic, pro-individual, anti-cant, and anti-elite. That seems inherent in the common practices of the form. Informal style cuts through the obfuscating generalities of creeds, countries, companies, bureaucracies, and experts. And narratives of the felt lives of everyday people test idealizations against actualities. Truth is in the details of real lives.

What a chasm seems to lie between these two worldviews. How modest Kramer's claim that the "literary journalist" might in some way act politically—act that way, in effect, by not acting that way, by not directly engaging the great forces that dominate our time. This is how many of the current generation of writers have lived, at least as writers. Or so it sometimes seems.

One would never want to say that writing has not played a part in great events, but its power to do so has never been straightforward or certain. James Agee's *Let Us Now Praise Famous Men* is a book of social protest, an enduring portrait of the miseries of Depression-era southern sharecroppers. It is felt to be a classic now, but was ignored during the era it describes. Even John Milton could go unheard in his time. *Areopagitica*, his eloquent plea for freedom of expression, was addressed directly to the British Parliament, which, we are told, ignored it. But countless writers of the past clearly believed in the *possibility* of affecting their times through writing. Certainly some modern nonfiction writers lack that faith—or have been cured of it. But not all, and many who may indeed lack the faith still strive to write "politically." The essayists who publish their reasoned protests in small-circulation magazines, for instance. Or the journalists who believe that recounting the experiences of individuals is one powerful means of describing the real costs of an era's social ills, and who feel that even if their protest isn't heard, it will be lodged; that there is value in "bearing witness."

In 2012, an American writer named Katherine Boo published a book about a slum called Annawadi, situated near the international airport and opulent hotels in Mumbai. The book, *Behind the Beautiful Forevers,* is built on the intersecting stories of several families and individuals in the slum: garbage pickers, petty thieves, worried parents, all victims of gruesome poverty and outrageous injustice. This is difficult material transformed by story, by Boo's skill in making those unfortunate people real— people with hopes and plans and flaws and virtues, all looking for ways to improve their lives, people at bottom not all that different from anyone else, people the reader roots for and occasionally against. One hardly notices while reading their stories that the author is also supplying some of the sociopolitical context in which the stories occur, not a sanitized but a distilled context, so lightly insinuated that we *feel* we understand the forces that afflict these people.

It is only at the end of this book, in her "Author's Note," that

Boo addresses us directly. We learn that she spent almost four years in Annawadi, conducting, among other things, both interviews and door-to-door household surveys. (The "vagrant sociology approach," she calls this. She also collected, laboriously, more than three thousand official documents.) She allows that the story of one slum can never be called "representative of a country as huge and diverse as India." But, she writes, "I was struck by commonalities with other poor communities in which I've spent time." She writes briefly but persuasively on several big subjects in this note—about corruption, for instance, telling us that one of its great and underacknowledged effects is "a contraction not of economic possibility but of our moral universe."

And she also tells us her intentions: "When I settle into a place, listening and watching, I don't try to fool myself that the stories of individuals are themselves arguments. I just believe that better arguments, maybe even better policies, get formulated when we know more about ordinary lives." This is one contemporary author's "Why I Write." Her approach is different from Orwell's but the spirit is much the same. She too, it seems, is trying to make political writing an art.

The passage from Orwell and the contemporary code expressed by Kramer—"Truth is in the details of real lives"—represent a spectrum of possibility for a writer. No one should presume to tell anyone where to fit on this spectrum, but one should recognize that it exists. Even those who have been trained in a language of distance and irony toward everything institutional, and especially toward government, must feel from time to time that there is something that justifies thinking in Orwell's terms—that there is something about one's own time that demands response. But what response, and how to make it? One can only say it is possible that writers live most fully when their work moves beyond performance, beyond entertainment or information, beyond pleasing audience and editor, when it does all that and yet represents their most important beliefs.

6

THE PROBLEM OF STYLE

═══════════

H. W. Fowler's Modern English Usage *belongs on every writer's shelf, and there it was on mine, but the book became a real presence in my life only when William Whitworth took over as the eleventh editor of* The Atlantic Monthly. *Whitworth had no connection with New England. He grew up in Arkansas and still had the soft accent of the region, and he had previously worked as a senior editor at* The New Yorker, *but in a way he was more Boston than Boston itself, proper and punctilious. Before Whitworth, most of the editors concentrated on politics, foreign affairs, literary trends, and long lunches, not always in that order. The finer points of grammar and punctuation were handled on another floor. But under Whitworth, commas became everybody's business. He quickly became known for his acute, if sometimes demoralizing, marginal comments on proofs. He wrote with a mechanical pencil in a tiny but astonishingly legible hand. Most maddening of all was his occasional apology—"I'm reading fast"—appended to an observation that most editors could not have made if they had taken all day. His comments often concerned subtle grammatical violations, and after noting one, such as "a possessive can't be an antecedent," he might add, "See Fowler." "See Fowler" became a popular sotto voce mutter among the temporarily traumatized staff.*

We had not thought ourselves in need of reform, but a reformer was upon us.

Kidder ran afoul of Whitworth's pencil more than once. He (that is, Kidder: a possessive can't be an antecedent, remember?) submitted his first manuscript of the new regime on "corrasable bond," the thin paper that once made life easy for erring typists. "Never again this paper, please," said the tiny handwriting, darker and more emphatic than usual and suggestive of strong feeling. Kidder, no doubt encouraged by my grumblings, had already formed a low opinion of the interloper who was threatening the clubhouse good spirits of the magazine where we had both been trying to make our mark. Kidder did not take this rebuff well.

The Atlantic *was to publish an excerpt, actually a condensation, of his forthcoming book,* The Soul of a New Machine. *This was logical—not only was it an Atlantic Monthly Press book, but it had virtually been written in the offices of the magazine—and it was also good news for the book's prospects. By this time, the book had been copyedited, but it still had to go through the magazine's own routine. Kidder's galleys now faced Whitworth's scrutiny.*

A number of issues came up, but the one I remember best had to do with an indelicate quote. A computer engineer was quoted as saying of the new machine he was designing that it would go "as fast as a raped ape." Whitworth struck the line on grounds that it was vulgar, which, of course, it was. But was that sufficient reason to deny the writer the use of it, given the distancing effect of quotation marks? And (my immediate concern) how was Kidder going to react to this proposition?

There are two kinds of dog. One will drop a stick at your foot. The other will clamp down harder on the stick the more you try to pry it out of his mouth. Reporters tend to be the second kind of dog. Kidder is ordinarily quite open to suggestion, but it was clear that he did not want to let go of his quote, and he resented the assumption that he would do so.

I was caught in the middle. On the one hand, one would not want to lose one's life or job, or even a night's sleep, defending the phrase "raped ape." On the other hand, this was my writer, and the quote was the quote and it was only a quote, and to lose it would leave a hole in the scene. It did seem to me that the dignity of the magazine could survive our printing the distasteful words.

Whitworth was so exercised on the point that he had devoted a long sardonic marginal note to imagining the sort of person who would use the phrase. He said among other things that it sounded like a college sophomore who had bongo drums in his room and fake African tribal masks on his wall (admittedly a telling argument).

But we were not the people who used it, I argued.

But by implication we were, Whitworth countered. Our use of it, he said, was "endorsive."

What does he mean by that? said Kidder, in a more emphatic way. Where did he come up with that word?

In the end the quote did not survive. Whitworth showed no sign of yielding and Kidder, though not convinced, stopped insisting. Was the right thing done? It's certainly true that Whitworth was trying to protect the elegance of his new magazine's pages. But he also had a point, which we might have seen more clearly had antler bashing not been involved. Out of curiosity I recently looked back at the passage in question. It was one in which Kidder describes his subject in a way that was clearly meant to make the engineer sound interesting to the reader.

If the reader thought the author was impressed with the wit of "raped ape"—well, that would indeed have been "endorsive," and bad news for the author.

This miniature moment suggests the varieties of ways in which the style of a piece of writing is formed—the choice of a quote, a single word, the honoring or dishonoring of a grammatical nicety. We think of an author's style as if it were some sort of fixed identity, but it is made up of an accumulation of granular decisions like this one. I remember once in those early days giving Kidder some advice about style. I said in effect, "Look, you are not always the calmest and most reasonable person in the room, and there is no need to be. But you admire such people. Why don't you just pretend to be a reasonable man in your prose?" I think it was useful advice, actually, but it's not as if a style is a one-time discovery. It is created and re-created sentence by sentence, choice by choice.

Whitworth and Kidder ultimately made their peace and became friends. One day years later, in a different situation, Kidder and I found ourselves wondering without irony if the use of another questionable quotation sounded "endorsive." Meanwhile, The Atlantic under Whitworth's direction went on to become what was, at least at the level of sentence and paragraph, the best-edited magazine in America.

A couple of H. W. Fowler's more eloquent pronouncements appear in this chapter. Perhaps they will win some more converts. Really, every writer who doesn't already have one should buy a copy of Modern English Usage. Note that I said "buy," however, and not "purchase." No one who has read Fowler on "genteelisms" will ever again use "purchase" as a verb.

—RT

"Omit needless words" goes the advice from *Elements of Style,* by Strunk and White, and no one would disagree. On the other hand: How do you recognize a needless word? Should Lincoln have written not "Four score and seven" but "eighty-seven"? In King Lear's dying speech—"Never, never, never, never, never"— which word would you cut?

The familiar rules about writing turn out to be more nearly half-truths, dangerous if taken literally. They are handy as correctives, but not very useful as instruction. The authorities say to avoid the verb "to be" and the passive voice, and to write with active verbs instead. Sit down at a desk declaring, "Today I write with active verbs," and you will likely end up in parody or paralysis. But notice that a paragraph depends too much on the verb "to be," and you may open a route to revision.

The verb "to be" and the passive voice are unfairly maligned. God invented both for a reason. Just turn to the Bible: "In the beginning was the word, . . . and the word was God." No one would accuse that verb of weakness. Or Shakespeare: "There is a tide in the affairs of men / Which, taken at the flood . . ." (the verb "to be" and the passive both). Occasionally the supposed weakness of a verb can accentuate the nouns around it. Hemingway demonstrates this throughout his work. Any writer should use "to be" forms without apology when defining, or naming, or placing something. Consider the passive voice when the thing done is more important than the doer. Don't lean on these usages, but don't contort your prose to avoid them, either.

"Never use a five-dollar word when a fifty-cent word will do" said Mark Twain, and this advice seems to be universally accepted. True, there is no faster way to make a passage impenetrable than to accumulate long Latinate words. But much of the force of English derives from the conquests and invasions that gave it multiple sources. It is almost impossible to write prose in English without blending short, blunt Anglo-Saxon with more formal Latinate words, and the way you blend them matters. It is a little-noted fact that a reader's eye, just glancing at a page, can tell something about the contents simply by registering its texture. The mere look of your prose can invite readers to go on, or can warn them off before they read a word.

Great writers across the centuries have found their own ways to exploit the great variety of sounds available in English. Take for instance these lines of Emily Dickinson:

> Presentiment is the long shadow on the lawn—
> Indicative that suns go down—
> Notice to the startled grass—
> That darkness is about to pass.

A vigorous hybrid diction enforces the natural rhythms of English. So do be wary of an abundance of Latinate words, but don't automatically favor shorter words.

Although many are simplistic, all rules of writing share a worthy goal: clear and vigorous prose. Most writers want to achieve that. And most want to achieve something more, the distinction that is called a style. It's an elusive goal, but the surest way to approach it is by avoiding the many styles that offer themselves to you. The world brims over with temptations for the writer, modish words, unexamined phrases, borrowed tones, and the habits of thought they all represent. The creation of a style often begins with a negative achievement. Only by rejecting what comes too easily can you clear a space for yourself.

Some modes of writing are so familiar that they fall easily into categories. Let's take four of them, starting with the language in which so many writers have begun their professional education:

JOURNALESE

Daily journalism offers invaluable lessons in the venality of human nature and in the universal logic of politics, and also skills of great value to all nonfiction writers: getting facts right, saying no more than facts support, and writing fast. But reporting the news, especially on tight deadlines, is a specialized form of expression, a style of its own that finds its way into kinds of writing where it doesn't belong.

It's as if the world of news is governed by special physical laws. Things *skyrocket* or *soar,* or they *plummet* or *plunge.* They *slam into* other things (airplanes into mountainsides, hurricanes into shores). If many journalistic clichés are dramatic, others are unnecessarily cautious. In journalese, events seldom cause one another; they tend to happen *in the wake of* other events. Sometimes events simply happen *amid* other events, "amid widespread charges of corruption" or "as corruption charges *swirl.*" These clichés get used for a good reason: that cardinal virtue of journalism, of not overstepping one's bounds. But the writer unbound by newsroom conventions can avoid such stale evasions.

It is a premise of newswriting that "space is tight." Sometimes it is, sometimes not, but by convention it always is, and so methods for compressing language have become conventional, too. Possessives replace prepositional phrases: "Chicago's O'Hare," "New York's Central Park." Nouns are used as adjectives: "Novelist William Faulkner" (or "Nobel Prize–winning novelist William Faulkner"). Similar identifiers become slightly absurd: "Motorist Rodney King," "Missing Mom Susan Powell," "Two-time Grammy nominee . . ." Many writers outside of newsrooms have adopted this construction, maybe in an effort to seem official or urgent.

There is no need to rush. Give everything the time it deserves. Here is a very slow sentence from an article by Janet Malcolm in *The New Yorker*, a magazine that has long stood watch against journalese: "On the second day of David Souter's appearance before the Senate Judiciary Committee, in September, 1990, Gordon Humphrey, a Republican senator from New Hampshire, with something of the manner of a boarding school headmaster in a satiric novel, asked the nominee, 'Do you remember the old television program *Queen for a Day?*'"

This sentence doesn't have much urgency. In fact, it has a studied leisure, but one senses that the author is up to something. Here is the sentence rewritten in journalese: "*'Do you remember the old television program* Queen for a Day?' *asked headmasterly New Hampshire Republican senator Gordon Humphrey of then nominee David Souter at his September 1990 Senate Judiciary Committee confirmation hearings.*" That's about half the words of the original, and with the pertinent information up front. The facts are all there, but the tone is gone. And if you listen to these sentences, you realize that the original has the motion, let's say, of a woman bending over gracefully to pick something up, while the other is more like a woman falling down stairs.

That's the real problem with these sentences filled with nouns as adjectives—not that they violate a grammatical rule, but that they violate normal rhythms of speech. Good readers and good writers use both eyes and ears. And for a reader who hears the words, the shorter sentence actually takes longer to register. It is hard to hear, and thus the reader resists it. Sometimes longer is shorter.

The habit of compression, along with the exigency of a deadline, can lead a reporter to insert information into a sentence randomly, as if tucking in loose shirttails. Let's say you're writing a story about a drug bust that involves a young mother from Indiana. In the lead you establish that the woman, named Polly Wabash, is being held for possession somewhere in Ohio and that she denies the charges. But you look back and see that you didn't give her age. So in the next paragraph, when you quote her, you make a small addition: *"I have no idea how that stuff got into my car," said the twenty-eight-year-old.*

Or, if you've forgotten something else: *said the twenty-eight-year-old Indiana native.*

Shirttail tucking can happen in a small way, with the use of an adjective to convey information that might otherwise require a sentence. The sports reporter, instead of saying that a certain player is injured, compresses the information to *the injured Gronkowski.* Similarly: *the vacationing Smiths, the breakaway re-*

public, or even the very common *in nearby Park Ridge.* None of these usages is wrong, and yet they all subtly lower the tone of a sentence.

Such alterations can get very subtle indeed, as in the following made-up passage: *A forty-year-old New York man was held today on charges of public indecency. Henry Hudson was arrested while buying a pair of shoes in a midtown department store.* By convention we know that "the New York man" is one and the same as "Henry Hudson." But nothing in the syntax says that. Logically, we would be justified in thinking that we were reading about two different people.

It is possible to be a journalist without sounding like a newspaper.

THE NEW VERNACULAR

Writing in the vernacular has produced some of the glories of American prose. "All modern American literature comes from one book by Mark Twain called *Huckleberry Finn,*" said Hemingway, celebrating that distinctive strain in our writing that makes the diction and rhythm of common speech into art. From Huck to Holden Caulfield and beyond, the vernacular has been the expression of youthfulness, both literally and in the broader sense of freshness and impatience with convention.

Of course the unconventional can become conventional, and quickly too, and that seems to have happened in the new vernacular. An aggressive informality infects contemporary prose. The Internet has helped to spread it; informality is the natural voice of the blogger. Here is an example from a blog much loved by solvers of the *New York Times* crossword, *Rex Parker Does the NY Times Crossword Puzzle*. In this quotation, Rex is away and his friend "PuzzleGirl" sits in:

> Well hi there! And Happy New Year! Bet you didn't think you'd be seeing PuzzleGirl again so soon, did you? Neither did I. It's a long story and it's not very interesting so I won't bore you with it. I'll just say that it involves Rex becoming unsure about which day it was yesterday. It actually sounded a *little* like some kind of alcohol-induced confusion but I don't really have anything to base that on. Total speculation. Absolutely no facts.

This is fun and highly readable. Like its antecedents, the new vernacular represents a democratic impulse, an antidote to vanity and literary airs. It's friendly, it's familiar. But familiar in both senses. The new vernacular imitates spontaneity but sounds rehearsed. It has a franchised feel, like the chain restaurant that tells its patrons "You're family."

In part this is just a matter of cliché. Some writers try to casualize their prose with friendly phrases such as "you know" or "you know what?" Or even "um," as in "um, hel-lo?" The op-ed columnist, repeating a point for emphasis, says, "Oh, and did I mention?" The blogger's beloved initialisms, such as "OMG," "LOL," "OTOH," now find their way off the screen and into type. "Whatever" serves to dismiss an argument. Or maybe just "Duh."

The new vernacular writer is studiedly sincere. Sincere even when ironic, ironically sincere. Whatever its other goals, the first purpose of such prose is ingratiation. Of course, every writer wants to be liked, but this is prose that seeks an instant intimate relationship. It makes aggressive use of the word "you"—"bet you thought"—and even when the "you" is absent, it is implied. The writer works hard to be lovable.

The new vernacular prose is studded with amiably self-questioning qualifiers, such as the all-purpose "kind of," especially useful as a modifier of otherwise extravagant remarks. Things aren't wrong, they are "kind of heinous." Things aren't good, they are "really sort of magnificent."

These last usages are, far from being street talk, the vernacular of a branch of the intelligentsia. The late David Foster Wallace entitled an essay on contemporary fiction "Certainly the End of Something, One Would Sort of Have to Think." Wallace was both a supple and complicated thinker, and a master of the self-effacing mode, his busy mind darting easily from slang to hermeneutics. In fact, a writer in *The New York Times*, Maud Newton, traced the origin of "the whole thing," a favorite phrase of his, to Wallace. The problem with "the whole thing," she allows, lies not with the brilliant Wallace but with his imitators, who mimic his tics but lack his intellect. And they are legion.

Breeziness has become for many the literary mode of first resort, a ready-to-wear means to seeming fresh and authentic. The style is catchy, and catching, like any other fashion. Writers should be cautious with this or any other stylized jauntiness— especially young writers, to whom the tone tends to come easily. The colloquial writer seeks intimacy, but the discerning reader, resisting that friendly hand on the shoulder, that winning grin, is apt to back away.

INSTITUTIONALESE

To those who weigh in on styles of American English prose, the archvillain is the anticolloquial mode, the megaphone of The Organization. If the person behind the colloquial style sounds a little too perky, there appears to be no person at all behind institutional prose, typically the language of concealment and pomposity. Its characteristics are well known, much maligned, and therefore, one would incorrectly think, generally avoided.

Institutionalese tends to obscure responsibility for what is being said, or to locate it in a heavenly source. One hears that old bugaboo, the passive voice: "Mistakes were made"; "Actions will be taken." Everyone recognizes the phenomenon. Why does it continue? The skeptical reader will credit the offending writer not with ineptitude but with a positive talent for obfuscation. The annual report writer declares, "Year-end results were negatively impacted by seasonal downward profit adjustments, consistent with global trends, insufficiently offset by labor force reductions." It's not that the guy doesn't know how to say, "We lost money last fall, fired some people, but it was a tough year all around." He either doesn't want to say that, or, more likely, would get fired if he did. Sometimes people simply have to give the appearance of saying something without the risks that come with doing so. Then prose becomes dowdy clothing, concealing more than it reveals.

One expects this kind of prose from governments and corporations, but the academy produces some wondrous examples too, prose that is opaque unto incomprehensibility. Here is a sentence from a highly respected literary scholar, published in the journal *Diacritics:*

> The move from a structuralist account in which capital is understood to structure social relations in relatively homologous ways to a view of hegemony in which power relations are subject to repetition, convergence, and rearticulation brought the question of temporality into the thinking of structure, and marked a shift from a form of Althusserian theory that takes structural totalities as theoretical objects to one in which the insights into the contingent possibility of structure inaugurate a renewed conception of hegemony as bound up with the contingent sites and strategies of the rearticulation of power.

This is not a parody, just an extreme example of its type. The passage, published several years ago, achieved a certain immortality when it won first prize in a "bad writing" contest sponsored by another journal, *Philosophy and Literature.* The sentence is notable for its reliance on academic jargon, but even without understanding its meaning, one can sense that revision would help. Indeed you want to save the sentence from itself, to suggest, perhaps, that the writer shorten the distance between the first subject and its predicate (thirty-three words). Often one of the most helpful things an editor can say to a writer is, "Make this two sentences." In this case the answer would probably be more like five. Not that one would want to put a word limit on sentences. Some great writers (Marcel Proust and Virginia Woolf, for instance) have spun them out at impressive length. But clarity can sometimes be achieved simply by giving every idea a sentence of its own.

Much overstuffed prose reflects a desire to bully, to impress, or to hide. And yet it must be granted that some writers in this mode do not really find themselves in the morass by choice. Some are actually trying to be clear, even literary. What makes them fail? Inflation of language is sometimes not a boast but a cosmetic for insecurity. It takes some confidence to write clearly.

Certain constructions attract writers in hiding. One, at least, is old enough for Fowler to have given it a name: "the sentry clause." He describes it under the heading "PARTICIPLES. 4. Initial participle &c." The passage reads in part:

> Before we are allowed to enter, we are challenged by the sentry, being a participle or some equivalent posted in advance to secure that our interview with the C.O. (or subject of the sentence) shall not take place without due ceremony.

A contemporary example of the sentry clause might go something like this: *A longtime student of history, he entered politics as a state representative at age thirty-five.* There is nothing grammatically wrong with this sentence, but it betrays a desire on the part of the writer to sound serious or literary at the expense of clarity. It is unlikely that the writer would ever speak such a sentence in conversation. But to the uncertain stylist, simple declarative sentences sound insufficiently important.

The initial dependent clause is a dubious construction under the best of circumstances. A sentence built on it is usually weaker than a straightforward declarative sentence. *A devoted husband, he bought her a diamond bracelet.* The usual problem is that the reader expects the clause to be logically connected to the statement that follows, but the nature of the logic is fuzzy. Do diamonds suggest devotion, or does the guy have something to hide?

Things get worse when the two parts of the sentence don't connect at all: *An avid duck hunter, he likes opera and soft porn. An Indiana native, Polly is the mother of three.* Does the writer mean to suggest that Hoosiers are naturally fertile? Obviously not. Readers aren't supposed to think anything. It only sounds as if they are. The ghost of logic haunts these constructions. They have been around for a long while, but tradition does not validate them.

The nervous writer is also likely to exhibit a morbid fear of repetition. Here is a recent candidate for the presidency, Governor Rick Perry of Texas, struggling for gravitas: "Even if someone is attracted to a person of the same sex, he or she still makes a choice to engage in sexual activity with someone of the same gender."

In cases like this, the effort to avoid repetition only calls attention to itself. Here, too, Fowler can be helpful, with his term "elegant variation," which sounds like a compliment but isn't. Fowler writes of this error with evangelical feeling, both excessive and splendid:

It is the second-rate writers, those intent rather on expressing themselves prettily than on conveying their meaning clearly, and still more those whose notions of style are based on a few misleading rules of thumb, that are chiefly open to the allurements of elegant variation. . . . There are few literary faults so widely prevalent, and this book will not have been written in vain if the present article should heal any sufferer of his infirmity.

What is elegant variation? Suppose you are writing about housing prices in Boston and you say, "Houses on Beacon Hill without exception list above seven figures, but the occasional residence in Back Bay can be found for under a million dollars." Expressing "a million" in two different ways isn't confusing, but the careful reader might well wonder whether you are making a distinction between "houses" and "residences." The second word stands out because the reader suspects it is there only to avoid being the first. But the reader can't be sure. You could be fudging the statistics, for instance, to include lower-priced apartments as "residences."

Finally—finally at least for a short list—the pompous but self-doubting writer has a penchant for overfamiliar metaphor, sometimes for multiple familiar metaphors. *We need to grease the skids if this project is ever going to catch fire and take us to the Promised Land.* When metaphors are fresh they are a form of thought, but when they are stale they are a way to avoid thought. *Tip of the iceberg* offends the ear as a cliché, and it offends reason because it is imprecise, if not spurious—just as when people say, "And the list goes on," and one knows that they have actually run out of examples. Often the writer will try to excuse the cliché by acknowledging it ("the proverbial cat that ate the canary") or by dressing it up ("the icing on the marketing cake"). These gambits never work. A cliché is a cliché. Orwell took a hard line on tired metaphor. In "Politics and the English Language" he wrote, "Never use a metaphor, simile or other figure of speech which you are used to seeing in print." One wouldn't want to forbid writers from using the occasional ancient phrase—*a dog in the manger* or *the boy who cried wolf*—but on the whole, Orwell gives sound advice. The mind that relies on cliché does not really know what it is saying.

But read the pompous writer with sympathy! A scared and a confused creature lurks behind the self-important drone of that voice. He is hiding things from the reader but also, in all likelihood, from himself. And if you should find yourself sounding that way, ask yourself what you are trying to avoid.

PROPAGANDA

Ever since Orwell's novel *1984*, the world has had a keener ear for the manipulation of vocabulary in the service of ideology or of the state. It is not unusual in any political contention to hear one side or another accuse the opponent of "Orwellian" language, the blatant distortion of meaning to benefit one's position. Ongoing debates are framed in self-serving terms, and these terms are depressingly effective at preventing discussion. Early in the game, the abortion controversy froze into a dualism: "right to life" vs. "freedom to choose." In 2011, the debate over marginal tax rates created two loaded ways of characterizing rich people: "America's most fortunate" vs. "job creators." If you feel passionately about one side or the other in such debates, fine; only you must not succumb to the language that seeks to persuade merely by naming.

The most dangerous propaganda is that which one fails to recognize—the language that insinuates itself into the general consciousness, language that seems to represent consensus but, on a closer look, obscures differences. This is the language that truly blocks understanding.

Let's take a single word much with us in early-twenty-first-century America: "terrorism." Objecting to a word is usually a fool's game. There are no bad words, only bad contexts. The most vulgar obscenity can be made tender by lovers; the worst racial epithet can be tamed by its victims. But since the destruction of the World Trade Center, "terrorism" has come about as close to a bad word as the American language contains. Bad in its imprecision, its unexamined premises, its power to confuse, its unique ability to demonize.

"Terrorism." This big, capacious, amorphous word, big enough for everyone's hatreds and fears, has been used by so many people for so many ends that writers simply have to know what they mean when they use it, and somehow make that meaning plain to their readers.

The economy of words is a wondrous system. Language is free and available to all in limitless quantities, an utterly democratic commodity. But as soon as you help yourself to this bounty you can begin to trade in your own identity. A great deal of the common language is borrowed without much thought from a part of the culture that may or may not represent the writer, a culture with which the writer may or may not want to be allied. Use enough words wantonly and you disappear before your own eyes. Use them well and you create yourself. This is why writers must own their language. Own your language or it will own you.

•

When quoting great writers we tend to use the present tense, even if they died centuries ago: "Milton reminds us . . ." "As Shakespeare says . . ." The literary convention recalls the truth that must have inspired it. Writers we revere feel like colleagues and confidants, as if they were speaking to us directly. This communion of strangers, living and dead, derives from the rather mystical quality called "voice."

The term "voice" appears constantly in criticism today. Sometimes people use it interchangeably with "style," but usually it is supposed to mean more, often nothing less than the writer's presence on the page. The term indeed may soon buckle under the weight it is asked to bear. Certainly it has become discomfiting to hear writers speak about their own voices. You cannot, must not, try to design and create a voice. The creation of voice is the providential result of the writer's constant self-defining and self-refining inner dialogue. When it happens, let someone else tell you, and be grateful.

Yet it is undeniable that good writing must have a human sound. Maybe that is the more modest word to keep in mind: sound. You try to attune yourself to the sound of your own writing. If you can't imagine yourself saying something aloud, then you probably shouldn't write it. That is not the same as saying, "Write the way you talk." If we all did that, civilization would be in even worse shape than it is. This is closer: Write the way you talk on your best day. Write the way you would like to talk.

Sometimes it will happen, in the middle of a difficult piece of writing, that one morning you wake up with a sentence in mind, and the sentence contains a sound that seems to unlock the problem for you. Speak to no one, go and write that sentence down. The sound can be more useful than a multipage outline. It is the sketch that precedes an architect's blueprints, the writer's equivalent of a vision.

So listen to yourself. And it helps to keep one's ear tuned to the great voices that have preceded us, not to copy them but to be inspired by them. Hunter Thompson once said that he taught himself to write by typing out *The Great Gatsby*. This seems touchingly innocent—and Thompson's choice of models is odd, given the turns that his own style took. But probably he wasn't so naïve as to think he was going to write like F. Scott Fitzgerald. Perhaps he knew that we all need writers from whom we learn lessons that go deeper than mannerism. Listen to yourself, and listen to those writers who are so great that they cannot be imitated.

7

ART AND COMMERCE

I recall, with a warmth I didn't feel at the time, the day in 1978 when great good luck descended on my writing career. By then I had written my bad unpublished novel and a bad but published book of nonfiction, which had received almost no reviews and had not sold enough copies to earn out the publisher's small advance. For about five years since then, I had been writing articles freelance for The Atlantic. I had just finished another article, a long one, and was sitting in Todd's office. I was drinking beer, a custom I had established for such moments, which Todd tolerated, I think, because he hoped that it would keep me from expressing my usual postpartum anxiety. I was broke, I explained once again. I was tired of writing articles. I wanted to write a book, a better book than I had written before. What could I write a book about?

Todd said, "Why don't you look into computers?"

I was afraid of math and science, and consequently I disdained the class of people who were competent with them. The prospect of looking into computers seemed daunting and drab, as drab as the word "engineering." I wish I could claim that I was the sort of daring young reporter who would press forward and let himself be proven wrong. In fact I took Todd's suggestion because just then I couldn't think of anything else to look into.

Three years later I had a book, The Soul of a New Machine. *Todd's idea turned out to have been, at the very least, timely. The personal computer did not yet exist. Computers were still curiosities, but they were arousing great interest, in part because the business in those machines was already producing vast amounts of wealth. The* Atlantic *published excerpts of the book, and, probably more important commercially, so did a trade magazine widely distributed among people involved in the computer business. Then the editors of* The New York Times Book Review *chose an engineer to review it—Samuel Florman, who had himself written a book called* The Existential Pleasures of Engineering, *and who was clearly delighted to read something that ran counter to what he felt was an antiengineering bias among the literati, delighted by a book that seemed to make a branch of his profession exciting. And the editors of the* Book Review *put Mr. Florman's review on the magazine's cover.*

I had high hopes for my book, but I had not expected any of that, or any of what followed. Nor had the publisher—Atlantic–Little, Brown. After the Times *reviews—there was a very kind one in the daily paper, too—the publisher sent me to New York to visit the many bookstores that were still arrayed along Fifth Avenue. But there were no books left to sign. All up and down the avenue, every copy had been sold. I learned that it would take weeks for more copies to be printed and delivered. I felt aggrieved, of course. Unreasonably aggrieved. The publishers had in fact made a substantial bet on my book, a bet against the odds, a roulette bet. How could they have been expected to foresee a skein of luck that would make their bet look small?*

Luck followed on luck, or possibly grew out of luck. My book won prizes. I like to think it was a good book, but I hope it does not seem ungrateful of me to say that, having served on prize committees since,

I know that choosing winners is often a negotiation, and that negotiations over matters of taste can end up awarding the prize to everyone's third choice.

At one of the prize ceremonies I met John Updike, who told me he had my book. "It's a nice book," he said.

I thanked him, then added, lying, "I don't take all this prize stuff too seriously."

He replied, "Don't."

I was only in my thirties. I tell myself that I was too young to follow his advice and to acknowledge what had really happened to me.

It is easy to believe in the power of luck when one's own luck is bad. Good luck tends to tempt fishermen—and even gamblers!—to credit their own abilities. But for writers, at least, antidotes are available. Think of all the books in the stacks of the world's libraries and the certainty that among them are masterpieces that no one has read in decades. Think of the many wonderful writers who haven't earned a living by writing. Anyone who does earn a living by writing, and does not acknowledge the power of luck, has to be deluded.

—TK

Sooner or later, all writers have to come to terms with the practical side of their efforts, with commercial success—achieving it or not achieving it, longing for it or scorning it, or simply trying to make an honest living in the literary marketplace. One contemporary writer, Lewis Hyde, in *The Gift*, has contemplated this topic in spacious terms.

Hyde argues that the artist, including the writer, is fundamentally at odds with the market economy. Many writers have

shared this flattering perception at one time or another, especially when their genius was invisible to editors or when the
book-buying public was indifferent to their wares. But Hyde el-
evates what could be taken as resentment to an ennobling truth.
He argues that art and creativity generally belong, or should be
understood as belonging, to what anthropologists call the "gift
economy," an ethos that lies in plainer view in places like the
South Pacific islands than in midtown Manhattan. Creativity, he
says, proceeds from two gifts: the gift of talent and the gift of
tradition, which informs and guides individual talent. And the
act of creativity is itself a gift, which can't be aimed at making
money but must be freely given.

Hyde's sanctification of the writer's role can cause discomfort,
especially to a writer with some experience in journalism. The
newsroom and the magazine office both offer quick lessons in
avoiding preciousness. Journalists aren't likely to talk about
"art" and "creativity." If they dare to boast at all, they're apt to
talk about being "pros." Norman Mailer defined a pro as someone who can work on a bad day. He was an artist who loved the
sense of himself as a pro. The motto on the pro's coat of arms
would be the timeless wisdom of Dr. Johnson: "No man but a
blockhead ever wrote except for money." A pro makes deadlines,
and a pro makes compromises, too. A pro lives in real time in the
real world and secretly relishes the constraints of the job. A pro's
greatest boast might be A. J. Liebling's: "I can write better than
anybody who can write faster, and I can write faster than anybody who can write better."

When writers convene they tend to talk in general ways about
the *business* of writing. Partly this is to avoid telling each other

what they really think of each other's work. But they do also seem genuinely unhappy with the institution they depend on, griping to each other about the malfeasance of publishers. No ads. No books sent to reviewers, or books sent to the wrong reviewers. No publicity. Or great publicity but no books in the stores.

Lewis Hyde seems to suggest that all of this is beneath a writer's dignity, that one should be suspicious of all marketplace success. But even ignoring such things as mortgages, it isn't clear that a writer of prose can easily separate art from commerce. The great prose art forms grew up in concert with the publishing business. Books must not only be written but must also be made, and historically the people who could make them soon became more than manufacturers. Publishers became arbiters of taste, of aesthetic as well as commercial value. This role endures, even as books become easier to produce and, thanks to electronic publishing, easier to distribute. Indeed its reputation as a judge of literary worth is a publisher's most valuable asset, which it is always in danger of squandering. Publishing is not an adjunct of culture but a part of culture, messy and venal as that culture sometimes is.

Traditional publishing depends on a basic triad of author, agent, and editor. For the intimidated young writer this relationship can seem nearly primal, yet another way to enact the classic family drama. The author, it goes without saying, is the child, the agent the supportive mother, and the publisher the father whose love must be won and won again by deeds alone.

For beginning writers the mystery of what happens inside publishing houses has for some time been preceded by the mystery of the agent. These middlemen/brokers occupy a central place. They serve publishers by finding and screening new talent and by collaborating in marketing, and, when things get tense, by serving as buffers between authors and editors. Agents can do some things that writers can't do for themselves. Most important, they can identify an editor who is apt to like a book. In publishing houses very few people have the power to say yes, but almost anyone can say no. So it is crucial to get a manuscript or proposal to an editor who is unlikely to shoot it down right away, who is likely instead to present it to colleagues with enthusiasm.

A young writer with a manuscript is often a bundle of apprehensions and ambitions, like a girl from the provinces coming to New York for the first time. (Sometimes the writer is exactly that person.) Braced for rejection, she can impute all sorts of qualities to the unseen powers. Why do some agents and publishers take so long to answer her e-mails and phone calls? Publishing is not an industry renowned for its efficiency. More than one writer has said ruefully, "The trouble with this business is that it's run by English majors." Which means of course that a lot of people in publishing resemble writers. This may be the beginning of wisdom. The people who write books actually have a lot in common with the people who produce and promote them. The sooner a writer can get inside the door and meet a few agents and editors, the sooner those people are revealed to be brothers and sisters—better dressed sometimes, though not always. Generally they are people who really do like books and are eager to make them better.

The book business is changing rapidly and unpredictably. For years it was accused of being old-fashioned, even ossified. Now people who work in publishing say they have no idea what it will look like in even a few years. But one essential truth is likely to endure. About 80 percent of the books that are published lose money. It may be that 80 percent deserve to lose money. Only a fervent believer in the sanctity of the market would imagine that it is the same 80 percent, but it is hard to imagine a future in which financial success will not be the exception.

So publishing seems bound to remain a gambler's business. Publishers, particularly of nonfiction books, are generally buying manuscripts that don't yet exist. They are taking a chance. Some publishers have stood by authors for years while waiting for books that might never be written or that might turn into something quite different from what was promised. But publishers are apt to behave like gamblers in another way as well. When a book doesn't sell, support for it in the publishing house tends to wane quickly. Editors cut their losses and turn their attention to other titles. Writers grieve when this happens, and sometimes they howl, sometimes with justice, crying, "If only, if only, they had tried a little harder to promote my book." It is cold comfort, but always worth remembering, that the alternative was for the publisher not to have taken a chance at all.

Writers starting out—and even successfully published writers—get all sorts of advice about marketing and "branding" themselves. They are told they must develop an "elevator pitch," a one-breath description of a book, said to be essential for sales. It can grate on the ear and the spirit to hear this, and to be told that to sell one's book, one needs a "platform"—some identity apart from one's role as a writer. The book proposal has become a minor genre of its own, like grant writing or the personal essay on college applications. There are even book proposal consultants and book proposal formulas. Authors are advised to create "marketing plans" to include in their proposals, and some dutifully spend weeks on the chore. Most of this is nonsense, and bad advice. A new writer should proceed cautiously, with a trusted agent's counsel, bearing in mind that the potential editor is primarily a reader, for whom the best marketing plan may well be twenty or thirty pages of good prose.

A writer who wants to write and to be published successfully has to try to cultivate a certain doubleness of being. When you are writing, you have to think of yourself as a writer and not as a commodity. But when your book is published, it becomes a product. Over the years publishers and agents have become increasingly sophisticated at promoting books, and to let pride keep you from cooperating in their efforts would be churlish and self-destructive.

In a magazine piece called "Hub Fans Bid Kid Adieu," John Updike tells the story of Ted Williams's last game, at Fenway Park. (In his final at bat, Williams hit a home run.) Updike tells us that Williams's detractors had long accused him of not being a "clutch hitter." Then Updike issues this rejoinder: "Insofar as the clutch hitter is not a sportswriter's myth, he is a vulgarity, like a writer who writes only for money." The remark is a corrective to Samuel Johnson's: Of course a writer writes for money, but only a blockhead writes *only* for money.

Everyone hopes for success. Somewhere along the way all writers experience rejection, too, and the pain it causes is real. But pain is a purer feeling than the despair, sometimes masquerading as hubris, that comes from equating one's self-worth with the size of a publisher's advance or even with the response of reviewers. It is self-defeating for a writer to live in a state of noble opposition to the business of publishing, and also self-defeating for a writer with literary ambitions to imagine that fortune is perfectly congruent with success. Some of what writers do, the best of it, is not easily or widely noticed. The deepest pleasure of a piece of writing may lie in a graceful narrative turn, an intuition about human behavior that finds exact expression, the spirit of generosity that lies behind the work. A good word for these things, when they occur, is "art." Whatever art any book achieves may or may not be rewarded in the marketplace, but art isn't generally achieved with the market in mind. Every book has to be in part its own reward. In happy moments one realizes that the best work is done when one's eye is simply on the work, not on its consequences, or on oneself. It is something done for its own sake. It is, in Lewis Hyde's term, a gift.

Surely most people have experienced this truth, even in humble circumstances. Success of this sort has a great deal to do with intention. A cook insists on a fresh herb, a carpenter repairs a piece of molding seamlessly, a radio journalist enlivens a report with a lyric phrase. It does not seem unreasonable to say that these gestures, these things that carry us beyond utility, that lie outside economic logic, are what make civilization worth inhabiting, and that their absence—which is frequent—can make the world a dispiriting place.

David Foster Wallace was admired by many of his fellow writers, and though his own highest ambitions may have been reserved for his fiction, some admired him as much for the witty, compulsively intelligent prose of his essays and reportage. At the New York memorial service for him, the novelist Zadie Smith quoted him as having said, ". . . the big distinction between good art and so-so art lies somewhere in the art's heart's purpose: the agenda of the consciousness behind the text. It's got something to do with love. With having the discipline to talk out of the part of yourself that can love, instead of the part that just wants to be loved."

8

BEING EDITED AND EDITING

===========

BEING EDITED
—*Kidder*

Editing isn't just something that happens to you. You have to learn how to be edited.

Some of the first editing I experienced was performed by students at the University of Iowa's Writers' Workshop. I went there in the early 1970s, a few years after the army, after I had written my Vietnam novel, which no one had published—which no one had published thank God, I say now. The Writers' Workshop seemed like a respectable escape from rejection slips for the short stories I had sent to magazines (one time someone wrote "Sorry" on the bottom of one of those printed slips, which made me feel both better and worse). More than that, Iowa looked like an escape from unemployment and various symbols of failure: the subscription to *The Wall Street Journal*, which a stockbroker uncle had bought for me uninvited, and the law school applications, for which in a weak moment I had written away and which my shy, laconic father had placed on the mantel in my childhood home, where I wrote most of my war novel.

At Iowa what was called a fiction workshop often felt like an inquisition, a dozen young writers in a seminar room, each with a copy of your story, all telling you what they thought of your creation. Withering comments were one thing: "pretentious," "sentimental," "boring," "Budweiser writing." But what made my heart sink were the transparent attempts at kindness, especially the line, "I'd like to know more about this character," almost always said of characters about whom any reader, even one's mother, would want to know less.

Young writers are unlikely to possess the modicum of self-lessness that a good editor must have, that makes it possible for one person to act in the best interests of another's work. Young writers, I think, are more likely to envy their peers or to disdain them out of self-disdain, and, worst of all, to be unaware of what they're doing. But I am speaking mainly for myself. In workshops I said harsh, dismissive things about other students' stories, precisely because they were no worse than my own, and sometimes because they were better.

I'm sure that for some of us young would-be writers the workshops were useful. Reactions varied. Some decided writing wasn't worth the pain and went on to other professions. Some actively defended themselves. I remember a young woman who, after her story had been pummeled a while, stood up and declared to the class, "This is a story about a lot of beautiful people and a lot of beautiful things *going down!*" and stalked out of the room.

The main lesson I absorbed had to do with standards for writing, especially for fiction. Mine had been both too high and too low. I had read great novelists and short-story writers, and imagined I would soon measure up to them. Now I realized I wasn't measuring up to some of the writers on the other side of the table. My solution was to submit as little as possible to workshops, and, after a while, to try my hand at nonfiction. No other students I knew were writing factual stories. Locally, I seemed to have the field to myself. Did I also sense that reporting might be good for me? In college once I had set out to write a novel but managed only about thirty pages, which I decorated with marginal comments and little drawings for my biographer to find. Brief forays into journalism felt like an escape from the sound of my own mind. I was forced to listen to other voices and to think about other lives. And I got encouragement from some of the faculty, especially from Dan Wakefield, a distinguished journalist turned novelist who had come to teach for a semester. Dan was a contributing editor for *The Atlantic*, and he put in a good word for me with Bob Manning. He also told me there was a smart young editor at the magazine named Richard Todd. I should try to work with him.

For months and months, Todd remained a voice on the phone, delivering bad news about my article on the mass murder case.

It didn't take me very long to fix the first problem, the problem of the opening sentence: "In the spring of 1971, someone went mad for blood in the Sacramento Valley." After only a few revisions the sentence read: "In May of 1971, the police in Sutter County, California, began to find men buried in the ground outside the town of Yuba City, in the central Sacramento Valley." Not a memorable sentence, but clear enough. And it no longer had the sound that I thought Todd meant by "melodramatic," drama supplied by the author, not the facts.

But Todd kept finding problems in my article. The largest

ones lay in my attempts to describe the murderer's trial, a long and tangled affair, most of which I had witnessed firsthand. How does one distill about a thousand pages of notes into a few pages of manuscript and manage to convey both the essential facts of an event like that and some of its flavor—its tedium, occasional drama, and weirdness? For starters, how to overcome the perfectly sensible conviction that this can't be done? Time after time, I rewrote, sent Todd the draft, waited a few days, then called him up, only to hear that my account was still, at best, confusing.

At first I felt like yelling at him: "Your reading is obtuse!" But of course I didn't yell. For a while instead I tried to use the kind of strategy too pitiful to be acknowledged while one is employing it: to make talking about what I had written achieve what my writing hadn't. Sometimes when he replied, there was a weary sound in his voice. Once or maybe twice, he made a short laugh, like a snort, to tell me, I sensed, that what I had just said was too preposterous for comment. But he never raised his voice. I would remember if he had.

I didn't keep the notes I made during those conversations or the many drafts I wrote of that article, drafts I never counted. No biographer sat beside me now. My adolescent dreams of writing something classic had turned into the necessity of writing something publishable. This was it for me. I really think I would have bought my own subscription to *The Wall Street Journal* if Todd had simply killed the article. As he should have done. As I would have done in his place. Months of reading the same old material from an all but unpublished writer, for an unimportant story. I never dared to ask Todd why he put up with it, but some years later, I raised the question with his wife, Susan, and she said, "He's willing to work as hard as the writer is."

Some of us writers come into the world believing that we are bestowing favors when we ask others to read what we've written. I like to think that during those many phone calls I began to learn otherwise—that when someone takes the trouble to read and respond honestly, I ought to feel grateful, even if I don't. But I did feel grateful, even jubilant, once the article was finally published, in a corner of *The Atlantic* called "Reports & Comment." Bob Manning said he was impressed with the work I had put in. He did not say he was impressed with the article itself. This was honest, not unkind. At the time, I didn't care. Publication was enough.

•

The kind of rewriting one learns, or used to learn, in high school or in a college freshman composition class, is a chore that mainly involves tinkering—moving sentences and paragraphs around, prettying up a phrase, crossing out words and substituting better ones. This is the kind of rewriting that the advent of word processing encouraged, by making it so easy. Not that finding the right word or eliminating the false note from a sentence isn't important. Sometimes tinkering reveals larger problems in a draft, sometimes even suggests solutions, but only if you're looking for larger problems and solutions.

I remember in college reading F. Scott Fitzgerald's unfinished novel *The Last Tycoon* and studying a note that he left in the manuscript: "Rewrite from mood. Has become stilted with rewriting. Don't look—rewrite from mood." I reread those lines so often, trying to understand them, that they stuck in my memory. Fitzgerald knew that there are at least two kinds of rewriting. The first is trying to fix what you've already written, but doing this can keep you from facing up to the second kind, from figuring out the essential thing you're trying to do and looking for better ways to tell your story. If Fitzgerald had been advising a young writer and not himself, he might have said, "Rewrite from principle," or "Don't just push the same old stuff around. Throw it away and start over." In any case, a lot of learning how to be edited was for me learning the necessity of this second kind of rewriting, which was most of what Todd and I did together for the next forty years.

On the phone he had become the voice that decreed failure or its opposite, which was publication. By the time I finally met him in person, he was authority for me. He could have been a giant or a dwarf, he could have worn a kilt or a pin-striped suit, and he still would have looked the part I had imagined for him—which is the reason, I suppose, that photographs of him from that time strike me as inaccurate. In fact, he was just a couple of inches below six feet, but I thought of him as small, because he was shorter than I. He looked like a prep school teacher or else a country squire, of the Protestant Irish type: ruddy skin, reddish sandy hair, khaki or gray flannel pants, a tweed sport coat, a functional necktie; all composed in varying degrees of rumpledness, which over the years came to seem admirably unselfconscious, because he clearly noticed the clothes that others wore, particularly women, whose dresses he referred to as "frocks."

I was twenty-seven and he was only thirty-two, but I recog-

nized him as a member of an older generation, an older generation, that is, of Americans who went to college before the
Vietnam War and the matriculation of the baby boomers, whom
Todd once described as "a generation of twits." He liked things
that seemed to me old-fashioned, such as farms and, at least hy-
pothetically, farming. He liked old buildings, bucolic landscapes,
antiques, and realistic fiction. And it seemed as if a lot of what he
liked he liked in opposition to what he didn't like, and I learned
more about the things he didn't like, many of which were things
I did like, such as exercise for its own sake, unrealistic fiction,
sunny climates, and cats. He was calm on the surface, and the
surface was what he let most people see; whereas I tended to
share my thoughts and especially complaints.

For about five years I worked with him on articles for the
magazine. I had only freelancer status, and I spent months re-
searching and writing articles for which I was paid at most a few
thousand dollars. I hadn't married rich. ("The hours are too long
at that business," my father used to say.) My wife had a modest
income, though, which allowed me the freedom to work under
Todd's tutelage. I didn't feel especially privileged, but of course
I was.

I called him at least daily when I was in the middle of writing
an article. On one of those occasions early on, I heard him clear
his throat, which seemed to mean that I had been talking for too
long. I hastened to explain that I wanted him to know as much
about the subject as I did. "But, Kidder," he replied, "I don't *want*
to know as much about it as you do." That article was about the
dumping of sewage sludge in the New York Bight, but I was
pretty sure this was a general warning. I got it, I thought. Part

of an article writer's job was to distill a lot of information not just for the readers but for the editor, too.

Often this was more than I could manage. Sometimes I came to Boston to finish articles, and Todd and Susan would put me up in their guest room—"the Ramada Room." (One of their daughters was slow to start the day; they called her room "room 17," as in, "There's trouble in room 17.") I spent two weeks at their place while working on my article about Vietnam combat veterans. According to Todd, I commandeered every evening, talking to him about something or other in that article: "I would be tired, I'd have to go to bed, and you would still be talking, and you would stay up God knows how much later, and the next morning I would be at the breakfast table, and you would come down the stairs still talking about that same thing in the article."

Being close by, getting glimpses of an editor's life, can give one a sense of an editor's problems and thus suggest ways to make oneself useful, and secure continuing attentions. But I suppose it could have worked the other way in my case. There were parties at *The Atlantic* and at Todd's house where I got drunk and made a scene. I committed some offenses that, no doubt for the same reason, I promptly forgot. Susan had an antique Toby jug, an English drinking vessel with a face molded into its surface. She kept it out of harm's way on a shelf in her kitchen. "You broke it," Todd told me, long after the fact. "It wasn't that you were looking at it. You were just . . . moving. And it fell. You as usual were frantically apologetic. 'Oh God. Oh God. Is this valuable?' Susan said, 'Oh, don't worry about it, Tracy. It's priceless.' That seemed to set you at your ease."

"Was I in my cups?" I asked Todd.

"It's not impossible."

Presumably, a writer and editor can work well together without sharing even so much as an occasional lunch, but I don't think editing from a distance would have served me well. At first, and for some years, I needed too much help, including reassurance, and by the time I might have needed help less, I was comfortable with things as they were. One evening he called my house, got my wife, and asked for me by saying, "Frannie, is your eldest home?" I wasn't offended, only amused, in part of course because I knew that amusement was his aim. He was playing the role of Todd. Ten years after we met, we were having dinner and I was lamenting that I was about to turn forty, saying how old it made me feel, and Todd looked up from his glass of cognac and said, "Kidder, I knew you in your thirties. And believe me, it is time for you to bid them adieu." I felt comfortable, comfortable unto complacent. I thought, "I'll remember that line."

By then we had many magazine articles and two books behind us. Habits, practices, principles, had accumulated into a small technology, our own peculiar ways of making articles and, especially by then, books.

What had worked for one occasion, we would say, probably wouldn't work for another. For instance, I wrote a magazine profile and later tried to use all of it in a book about the same person. The results were discouraging. After seeing a few revisions, Todd said, "You have to smash that article," and I imagined a porcelain cup lying on the ground in shards and saw myself picking up some of them, the curved part of the handle, a piece of the rim.

But in our practice, many general procedures have carried

over from one project to the next. I confer with Todd from the start, right from the opening question: what should I write about? The ideas for two books were his, and the idea for another came from Susan. Wherever suggestions come from, I discuss them with him, often for months, once for about two years. When I finally make a choice and begin my research, I tell him how it's going several times a week at least, unless the research takes me somewhere without phone service. His advice is a relief from the competing voices in my head, a place to begin or, once in a while, something tangible to argue with.

In our practice every book has seasons. After research comes the rough draft, the season that I dread. Once long ago, I set out after dinner to begin an article for *The Atlantic* and looked up to see daylight moving across a floor littered with crumpled balls of paper, at least a hundred versions of the article's opening sentence. For a time, I insisted that the first sentence be perfect before going on, and therefore spent whole days and nights getting nowhere. This sort of thing happened often enough to make me fear it. So I abandoned care entirely when writing rough drafts. Instead, I wrote fast. I would spend a day or two in reverie over my material, then scratch out a sort of plan, not even an outline but just a list of events, and then churn out pages as quickly as I could. Writing as fast as possible would prevent remorse for having written badly. I would take every path that looked interesting, and keep myself from going back and reading what I'd written, let alone trying to fix it. Meanwhile, I would try to forget the fate of previous rough drafts, the garbage bags full of paper, but of course I always remembered, so I'd tell myself that this time would be different, this time the rough draft would survive. But because I almost always lost faith in the draft long before I finished it, I would divide it into chunks. This also tended to foster speed, because the sooner I finished a chunk, the sooner I could apply for reassurance from Todd.

The rationale for this approach is that when you go out reporting, you always want to collect more material than you can use—far more, ten times more, a hundred times more. And then you want to audition a lot of that material on the page. So if you want to write more than one book in your lifetime, you have to write your first draft quickly. And anything I wrote that way, I found, was easier to throw away than stuff I'd labored over. Even the material that I had gathered and summoned up when my research seemed to be going badly, material I thought of as "good stuff," even that wasn't very hard to part with once I had written it up and seen it fail.

The cost of this approach is overstuffed, confusing first drafts, and, perhaps, an editor's consternation. "It might help if you thought things through before you start to write," Todd told me once, but only once, and then, I guess, he resigned himself to chaos. In the course of the immensely long first draft of my book *Among Schoolchildren*, I wrote the first few hundred pages in the first person, tried out an omniscient third person for the next five hundred or so, then went back to the first person for another long stretch, and wrote the last hundreds in something like the form of a play. Todd received photocopies of each chunk in turn. He let a few days pass each time, then said, as he always has, "It's fine. Keep going." And as always, I let myself imagine that he had actually read the pages, and also, so as not to feel I was a burden, that he hadn't. I have never asked if he actually reads my rough drafts. I don't want to know. The procedure works well enough. Why undermine its deep illogic?

I learned to like rewriting, maybe too much, but really it is the writer's special privilege. We rarely get the kind of chance in life that rewriting offers, to revise our pasts, to take back what we've said and say it better before others hear it. I usually write about ten more or less complete drafts, each one usually though not always closer to the final thing, like golf shots. This phase goes on for at least a year. I write and Todd reads and then we meet and talk about the draft, and then we do it all over again, again and again. Todd used to jot comments in the margins of the manuscripts for our meetings, but he would end up staring at the page, saying, "What did I write here?" Soon I was more adept than he was at deciphering his comments. But his penmanship deteriorated, and finally he quit using it altogether. Since then, the most I've found on pages he's returned are squiggly lines under sentences, which can mean any number of things, none of them good.

We've gone over manuscripts in restaurants, but a large private room is best. Todd likes to pace. I know we've made progress, that I am getting good at my book, when he says before a meeting that he wants to see the manuscript divided into all its pieces, spread out on a surface. A floor served for a decade or so, but a time came when a table was required, as the natural evolution of knees and backs made floors less accessible. Todd paces around the table, one hand in his trousers pocket, the other lifting piles of manuscript, as if to weigh them, while I take notes and work on keeping quiet.

Something is always wrong with a draft. I count on Todd to identify it. In the years of writing *Atlantic* articles, I sometimes felt that trusting him came at the expense of my independence, and back then I imagined that complete independence was a precondition for writing well, like getting drunk regularly and living in a garret. Sometimes I resented Todd's telling me that a character or incident or sentence was getting in the way and should be jettisoned. I told him I was going to compile a list of all "the good stuff" he had told me to cut. I never made up that list. I got only as far as remembering a man named Morris Kramer, a beachcombing "environmental activist" whom I had met in the course of research for my story on sewage sludge.

"You were completely fascinated by this guy," Todd reminded me. "But the guy really didn't have anything to do with the story."

I replied that the man was colorful.

"Yes," Todd said. "You had an interest in the colorful figure." My interest was enough of a problem for Todd to name it: "the Morris Kramer Problem." It's the problem of the irrelevant character, a dull cousin of the problem of the too-compelling minor character, the Mercutio Problem.

For the autopsy of a draft, we use the standard literary terms, such as "point of view" or "tone," and also terms of our own. "Exteriors" refers to anything that lies outside the story, anything that isn't direct observation of the characters and events. While doing my research for what became *House,* I found myself wondering where the lumber in the frame of the building came from. I followed it back, as it were, to the Big Woods of Maine: the logging camp where the trees had been felled and the mill where they were sawn. This was an exterior that seemed to fit within the narrative, and it survived. Most exteriors get cut, but they never feel like a waste of time. Not that this kind of research amounts to scholarship, but to write with confidence about a computer engineer's life for *The Soul of a New Machine,* I felt I had to learn a lot more than I would ever write about the history of computers, about the industry in general, about what was inside those devices. To write about Dr. Paul Farmer's work in *Mountains Beyond Mountains,* I had to understand, among other things, antibiotic resistance in tuberculosis. I read about it in medical texts, interviewed several specialists and a microbiologist, wrote and rewrote lengthy explanations, bored Todd and my household repeatedly with verbal explanations, and in the end Todd convinced me to boil it all down to a few sentences. The long versions got in the way of the main story I was telling, which was complicated enough: Farmer's discovery that poor patients in a Peruvian slum were being treated for drug-resistant tuberculosis in such a way as to induce further resistance to treatment. As for the full-blown exteriors that survive, the trick, we say, is to serve them up when a reader can be expected to want texture and context, or a break from the main story—that is, when the story would otherwise take on the tiresomeness of an excessively linear, one-thing-after-another narrative. An exterior should of course be interesting in itself. Like everything in a book of narrative nonfiction, it ought to serve at least two purposes, preferably unstated.

Sometimes parts of a story have to be "floated." This is short for "floated in time." You want, for instance, to describe the daily routine of a teacher, but you want to draw on observations that you made over many days. Perhaps many parts of many days were boring, but you never want to commit the imitative fallacy. You can certainly let the reader know a day was boring, but the last thing you want to do is bore the reader. You don't mislead the reader, though you may count on the reader's discernment. Sometimes signaling that a passage is being floated is as simple as moving from the past to the present tense, or using a phrase such as "day after day."

Floated things often serve as "timepassers." The term only sounds dismissive. "We need a timepasser here" is Todd's way of saying that the story needs to be slowed down or speeded up. It took the carpenters weeks to build the frame of the house that I wrote about in *House*, a period I especially enjoyed because the carpenters seemed to enjoy it so much and because the work site became so fragrant with freshly sawn wood. In the end, I described most of the framing in brief scenes interspersed with pertinent history, all meant to suggest the passage of time without replicating it. A timepasser is one possible means of "making some things big and other things little"—perhaps the most important phrase in our private lexicon. A timepasser can be a means of creating pleasing proportionality, of conveying, for instance, the essence of a weeks-long process like framing a house in fewer pages than you might give to describing a heated argument that lasted only minutes.

Things out of place or proportion give rise to a "bump," a term that I never liked to decipher in the margin of a page, back when Todd still wrote his comments. "A bump is worse than it sounds, isn't it?" I asked him once.

"Yes," he said. "It's not just something you drive over. It means these things in a story aren't connected, they aren't meshing, they don't meet. And so it gets you worried about the logic of the structure of the story."

"Taking the spin off" can be the solution not only to a melodramatic sentence, but to a problem of tone that infects a whole manuscript. A phrase like "someone went mad for blood" has, among its other demerits, a bossy quality. Taking the spin off can be translated roughly as: Don't try to *tell* the reader how to feel.

"You have to manage this" means something nearly opposite. Opposite also from the old saw "Show, don't tell," of which my college teacher Robert Fitzgerald once said, "It's a good rule, and it's meant to be broken." To manage something can mean slowing down an important scene to make it bigger than the things that are supposed to be little, and to do that you might try to find one moment in a story that can stand for many others. Or management might require a generalization, a summarizing statement that doesn't seem didactic. Todd calls this sort of statement "a brilliance," as in, "We need a brilliance here." He has supplied me with several over the years, phrases that I transposed a little or even used verbatim. In reference to the life of inmates in a nursing home in my book *Old Friends*, for instance: "The problem with visitors is they have to be thanked for coming and forgiven for going away."

Todd told me he didn't think editors should make up sentences for writers. "I've done it, but I don't like to do it," he said.

"But there are lines I've taken from you shamelessly. Ones you gave me in conversation."

"Well, conversation is one thing."

"What's the difference?"

"I don't know," he said. "Something mystical."

For years Todd prodded me to offer moments of generalization in the midst of a story or near its end. "How are we supposed to feel about all this?" he would ask me in our days at *The Atlantic*. I felt resistant usually, sometimes recalcitrant. I had long imagined that a story, even in nonfiction, ought to be its own best explanation. I still believe this. So does Todd, who puts the matter this way: "You want to avoid didacticism or a tone of insistence, or some form of allegory where people represent ideas." But at some point that I can no longer name, I understood that he was asking not for moralizing, not even for brilliances to put on the page, but for a sharpening of understanding. I began to feel that a successful narrative depends on buried generalization, on establishing a hierarchy of ideas—I picture one of Calder's hanging mobiles—to serve as the story's inner structure.

An abstraction can sometimes guide repairs to a part of a story that seems stubbornly inanimate. In draft after draft of *Strength in What Remains*, I wrote and rewrote the portrait of an ex-nun, to me a captivating character. The portrait lengthened with every rewrite. It had reached about forty lifeless pages when Todd's puzzlement lifted and he was able to give me both an estimate of the portrait's proper length—about fifteen pages—and also an idea to contain it. "Focus on the quality of her mercy," he said. Both kinds of advice usually help. Defining the length of a passage forces you to throw away the nonessential, and knowing the central idea tells you what to keep and where to put the accents.

Every story has special problems, and these usually get names, which I find reassuring—if a problem can be named, its solution can't be far away. "The problem of goodness" was Todd's phrase for the difficulties posed by the character Dr. Paul Farmer. Sometimes solutions can also be named. While writing *The Soul of a New Machine*, I worried and worried that I didn't know enough about the main character, Tom West, whose special vanity had been to make himself mysterious to me as well as to his team of computer engineers. Never mind, Todd told me. West could be brought to life partly through suggestive external details, and partly through other characters' perceptions of the man. Todd actually said, referring of course to F. Scott Fitzgerald's enigmatic title character: "That's all right. You can do a Gatsby on him."

The lingo that we now use over manuscripts preserves some of the remnants of books and articles past. To say "Which is fine" about matters that are decidedly not fine brings back the elementary school principal whose favorite line it was and the book in which he was a minor character. Likewise the carpenter who, on finishing a piece of clever joinery, declared, "Perfect or equal," and the nineteenth-century architect who drew up plans that would have had a building's top-floor windows sticking up out of the roof and who began his apology to the builder by saying, "I have made a sad mistake." Our talk has become infected with nostalgia, or, I prefer to think, maintains a sense of continuity. We have made sad mistakes before, which is fine, but we have always fixed them in ways that to us seem perfect or equal. We sign off sometimes with a line I heard back in Iowa City from the novelist Frederick Exley, who—long ago, half drunk in a bar at midday—told me, "This Iowa Writers' Workshop is an avoidance. It's a way of avoiding the *terribly lonely* and *deadly serious* business of getting on with it." Repeating the phrase—"Well, back to the terribly lonely business"—has been for me a way to make fun of those sentiments as if I've never fallen for them and before I have a chance to fall for them again. And they remind me that getting on with it has not been an entirely lonely business for me.

It has taken, on average, about three years for me to research and write a book, long enough for each to seem like an occupation in itself. A time has always come when I've wanted to quit that job and at the same time have been afraid of losing it. It would be worth having an editor if only to know when a book is finished. We used to go on a trip when Todd declared a book nearly done, with briefcases full of manuscript, in order to work without distractions. An inn in Maine in winter was the most productive setting, the most stimulating a hotel on a topless beach on St. Martin.

For the finish work, we set up what we call "watches." As I rewrite and he rereads, we keep an eye out for overused words and phrases. In one book the words "all right" were on the watch list; in another I had used "fluorescent" in almost every description of the story's setting. Repetitions, "reps," we long ago agreed, can be as destructive to a reader's confidence as, for instance, a flaw of tone or structure. And of all a story's problems, reps are the easiest to fix. The importance of the finish work, I think, is inversely proportional to the time and effort it usually requires.

When the page proofs come, we read the book aloud to each

other, pausing now and then to imagine bad reviews, an exercise in magical thinking—as if something imagined has actually happened, because, as everyone knows, fate abhors repetition, too. I recall, with an equanimity that was years in the making, an evening when he called to break the news that a very bad review had just appeared. What he actually said was: "Kidder, there was one review we forgot to write."

•

I suppose it is typical of human relations that I thought I knew Todd better in the first years of our collaboration than I think I know him now. The other day, for instance, he mentioned that he had met a mutual friend of ours while hitchhiking, and I was astonished.

"*You* were hitchhiking?"

"I was a hitchhiker," he said. "I once hitched across the country."

I couldn't reconcile the two pictures that entered my mind: my enduring picture of Todd the gentleman farmer in a rumpled tweed jacket, and this picture he drew of himself, lifting a thumb by the side of a road—though he allowed as how he had not worn a knapsack but had carried a leather valise. I was amused, of course, and I sensed a small unease under my amusement. I had the same feeling about his writing. He rarely mentioned it, and then one day by accident I found myself reading a short article of his in a magazine, an occasional piece in which Todd accompanies one of his daughters on a college tour. I read: "We met our tour guide, and then she asked us her name. 'Hi, my name is Melissa?'"

It was like hearing a very familiar voice in a crowd in a foreign city. It was as if he had been living another life, in secret. Granted I knew him as a person with a gift for privacy, but of course the secret was mainly my invention. I had an investment in a limited view of him. Over the years, I had done a Gatsby on Todd, unconsciously but on purpose.

For a long time, we played the parts of the libertine writer and the steady, Maxwell Perkins–like editor without literary ambitions of his own. Or rather, I enacted that cliché and he, I think, went along with it. I relied on what it gave me: the vital connection to an editor who I could plausibly imagine was right, almost always; and the avuncular friendship of an elder who possessed many qualities I lacked and therefore didn't have to cultivate, among them and above all, restraint.

Writers who need editors have to learn to listen, really listen, to advice that no one wants to hear—that you should jettison hard-earned pages, that you must start again. But how an editor delivers this advice makes all the difference, or has in my case, anyway. Every piece of writing, even classic works, can be ridiculed. So much the worse for nascent stuff by nascent writers. The risks at places like Iowa are premature development of the self-critical faculty and the loss of the unwarranted confidence that every writer needs. At least for some of us, being told a piece of writing stinks is the same as being told that we are once and for all bad writers, and therefore also deficient persons. It was decades ago when *The Atlantic Monthly*'s head editor, Bob Manning, scrawled his note to Todd, saying of me, "Let's face it, this fellow can't write." But Todd told me the story only recently. I guess he thought I was finally stable enough to take it.

He has never spoken harshly to me about a piece of my writing. I assume that he has always managed to say what he thinks, but he has done this gradually, in stages. "It's fine, keep going" for a rough draft is followed by, "Well, Kidder, this is progress" for a later one. He said once that he thought a writer—meaning me, I think—should learn to look at what he's written with "a little objectivity." Fair enough, but I think the ability to preserve the distinction between the writer and the writing is a skill an editor needs more than a writer does.

An editor of course has his own personality to accommodate while accommodating the often troublesome personalities of writers. There is something in Todd that keeps him from expressing a warm feeling outright, at least in public. Though I haven't often emulated it, I recognize that kind of reserve. I grew up surrounded by it, and as I grow older I find Todd's kind of reticence increasingly attractive. Whatever its origins, it usually functions as a form of courtesy, and in the special sphere of being edited, it has obvious value. Among other things, it assures you that your editor means at least as much as he says.

I like to remember the first book we worked on together, *The Soul of a New Machine.* Not just the book itself but also the time of working on it, and especially the final phase. It took place over perhaps a week, or maybe two, in Todd's office at *The Atlantic.* I loved that shabby-genteel place, especially after hours. Sometimes when I was there at night working on an article, I would take a break and wander the halls. The place was utterly still then and felt vast in space and time, the night watchman's marijuana smoke rising from the basement. I could wander into an office and gaze at framed letters from writers who had published in *The Atlantic*, studying the signatures of Twain and Emerson, Thoreau and Wharton, and dreaming.

That computers had not yet replaced typewriters was, in retrospect, a blessing. When the manuscript of *Soul* had improved enough to be considered a reasonable facsimile of a book, Todd and I spread its parts on the carpet in his office, as we had sometimes done for articles. Tall windows flanked the fireplace, shedding plenty of light on the piles of typewritten pages. Spreading the pages across the floor in itself lent the illusion of distance and control as we walked among the piles like a pair of Gullivers. In the afternoons, Heinekens helped us through the difficulties. Where should this thing really begin? Aren't the proportions off? Why do we give thirteen pages to that and only two to this? Now and then Todd picked a couple of pages off the floor for closer scrutiny, and said of some passage I had long admired, knowing it was grand and indispensable, "You could do without this." That was when I began to learn a skill which for me needs constant relearning, how to fall out of love with my own words. And, much harder of course, how to let go of some perfectly lovable words that nonetheless are at odds with the whole.

By the time we were done, Todd's office smelled a little like the inside of an old taxicab, but ashes still lay in his fireplace—it was late winter, I think—and the smell of creosote mitigated the odor of my incessant cigarettes. He squared up the edges of the tattered final manuscript and placed it on his desk. "Well, Kidder, this is a pretty good book," he said. "I don't think I've read another quite like it." High praise, the highest I have ever heard from him, or want to hear. In a week or two it would begin to wear off and I would start to wonder what he thought I should do next. For me, nothing much has changed since then.

EDITING
—*Todd*

I came to *The Atlantic* in the fall of 1969, three or four years before Kidder hove into view. He remembers me in those days as a tweedy, venerable, proto-curmudgeon. I remember myself as a skinny, bookish, and tentative youth, and I think an objective observer at the time would have sided with me.

I was quite taken with myself for having landed at this impressive magazine, but I was also intimidated by the job and by my colleagues. All magazines are dictatorships. Robert Manning ruled over this one, after a successful career at Time Inc. and a term as press spokesman for the State Department. He was used to places where things happened. He signed his memos with a big *M*. (Office manners dictated that the rest of us use our full set of initials in the lowercase.) Mike Janeway (mcj), to whom I owed my job, served as Manning's number two. Beneath Janeway, Michael Curtis and I occupied parallel rungs on the masthead. A strict hierarchy obtained. At one Christmas party a mischievous secretary read a poem she had written, a spoof on the old Boston lyric about the Cabots and the Lowells: "Here's to *The Atlantic* in Boston / Home of the bean and the cod / Where Todd and Curtis speak only to Janeway / And Janeway speaks only to Bob."

Manning, gruff and easily annoyed, cast a big shadow, but I

was in a way more intimidated by Janeway, my benefactor, who was my exact contemporary (and who became and remains my good friend). He had gone to Harvard, which (as he frequently reminded me) is a better place to have gone than Amherst, and this is especially true in Boston, where Harvard occupies the place that the University of Oklahoma occupies in Norman. Janeway knew a great deal more about the world than I did, and what he knew had already organized itself into a political philosophy. He had worked in the Senate as an aide to LBJ. He was brilliant, and he had connections. If he had been an object, he would been one of those old-fashioned telephone switchboards bristling with wires, most of them plugged into New York or DC. I once looked up from my desk to see a huge, stately, white-haired Dean Acheson under Janeway's care, like a statue being wheeled down a museum corridor.

My education had been narrowly literary. I had allowed myself to cushion my ignorance of the world with the idea that all politics were (was?—one never knows) not local but vulgar. I kept myself afloat by applying the reflexes of literary criticism to just about everything. I had an excessively scrupulous eye for style, a trait to which both education and instinct predisposed me. As far as it went, I guess it was a good eye. I did not succeed in bringing any names to the magazine. My fortunes seemed to rest entirely on my ability to fix things, and on my critical remarks on the yellow "comment sheets" that circulated among the editors with manuscripts under consideration. Without any particular convictions of my own, I developed a sense for the proper intonations of the center-left liberalism that the magazine stood for. By the time Kidder arrived on the scene I had been promoted, and sat in what was to be the nicest office of my professional life, the room, once the mansion's library, overlooking Marlborough Street. It had been the office of Charles Morton, the much-loved sidekick of the prominent editor Edward Weeks, in the 1940s and '50s. One day, when I was beginning to feel comfortable there, I encountered in the stairway a woman who had worked at the magazine for many years. She said, "Oh, hello there. I know who you are. You're the boy who sits in Mr. Morton's office."

Why is it so hard to summon a face from the past? When I try to picture Kidder in those days the first thing I see is a blue-striped seersucker jacket, a size too small for its owner, and in need of a trip to the cleaner's. He was big, well over six feet tall, lean but powerfully built through the shoulders. He had played football in high school. I don't mean that he advertised this fact. I came to learn it later, but it would not have been hard to imagine him on the playing field. He was expansive in gesture, given to waving his arms in explanation of an idea, and the space around him, whatever it was, always seemed too small to contain him. More than once over the years I have accused him of not sitting but falling into his chair (especially when I have had an interest in the chair in question). Yet this suggests a rather overbearing figure, and that wasn't the effect at all. He seemed oblivious of his size and force, stammered a bit when he spoke, and on the rare occasion when he took off his glasses, revealing circles of untanned skin, he would blink myopically. Above all, he seemed desperately afraid of giving offense.

I guess there was a time, as he suggests, when I was a more prominent figure in his life than he was in mine, but that was, as they say, destined to change. I didn't then but I now grow pumpkins in my leisure time. Pumpkin plants start out very small, and then the vines start to run and one day they cover the field. Kidder's presence at the magazine, and eventually in my life, was like that. He spread, and soon it was hard to imagine the world without him. He became in effect a staff writer, though unsalaried, and he was willing to take on almost anything. As we worked together, we became close friends.

On the surface we seemed quite different in temperament. Kidder had a gift for externalizing his anxieties, which allowed me to pretend to a tranquility I seldom felt. We had some vices in common and some interests beyond literary ones, notably sailing. He had the use of his father's sailboat for a week in the summer and we took a number of short cruises with our wives and another friend or two. Kidder was a good sailor, which meant you could relax on board knowing that the captain was unlikely to endanger your life, not always true in my sailing experience. *You* could relax, but he by nature could not, and his constant dithering was a source of amusement for his guests. Once, coming out of the Damariscotta River in Maine—into what was admittedly a shifting breeze—we changed jibs six times in about as many minutes. The beeriness of those days has been noted, but Kidder was what you might call an omniboire. It was not unusual for him during the course of a day to have a handful of beers, some Cokes, iced coffee, and a ginger ale or two before the anchor was down and it was safe to uncap the rum and uncork the wine. On the first trip we took we had to resupply after a day, and subsequently I took on the job of provisioning the boat.

Despite differences in style, we shared a code common to men of our era, which meant that we didn't expect much, or feel like offering much, in the way of confidences or confessions. Our dialogue was mostly made up of amiable insult. This mode of being is much lamented, but it is not entirely useless as a basis for lasting friendship, at least if you have time, and as it turned out we had decades.

The inherited idea of writer as reprobate and sot, editor as stabilizing influence, often undergoes modification in life. I remember a writer coming back from New York after an evening with his editor, who had not behaved well. The writer had to put the drunken editor into a taxi. The writer was quite disappointed by this scene. He thought that he was the one who by literary tradition was entitled to get drunk, and had been looking forward to it. In our case, Kidder may have been a more colorful drinker than I, but neither of us was unacquainted with the sauce.

Kidder in those days did, it's true, affect a certain air of dissolution and disarray. But, the reverse of Holden Caulfield's "secret slob," he was secretly organized. He was unfailingly punctual, for instance, and he had a virtue useful to a writer, a virtue he has never lost: an obsessive mind. It was clear from the start that he was going to be a writer. Successful or not, who can ever tell? But a writer. Over the years people have sometimes asked me what it "takes" to be a writer. When I answer this I start sounding like a basketball coach speaking of "desire." But, really, the answer is that it seems to take an inability to imagine yourself doing anything else—because anything else is so much easier. It would have been impossible to discourage Kidder, and heartless to try.

We have had some sport with Kidder's earliest work, the draft of his first magazine article and its lurid lead, and especially with the marvelously inflated novel *Ivory Fields*. In retrospect, though, these efforts are revealing. Why did his first article prove so stubborn? There was nothing wrong with the mass murder case as a subject. It was a fine subject for someone, but it was the wrong one for Kidder. It didn't fundamentally interest him. Years after I read *Ivory Fields*, after the merriment had died down, I found myself thinking of a line in it that was actually quite prophetic. The author says of his hero, the young lieutenant: "He is good, he is going to be brave, the night spills on him." Yes, this was inadvertently amusing, but from the start, I later realized, Kidder had an interest quite unusual for a writer, an interest in virtue. It's an immeasurably harder subject than vice. A bright thread of goodness runs through his subsequent books.

As I say, not easy to do. It was only when he was writing *Mountains Beyond Mountains* that I gave it the name "the problem of goodness." It's just as well that we weren't aware right away of this theme, preoccupation, instinct—whatever it was. And yet it's the kind of thing an editor should be looking for. An editor can serve a writer by being alert to his natural boundaries, his inner territory, his true interests.

I think Kidder's subjects understand his predispositions instinctively. Everyone can sense when someone is looking for the good within them, and it opens people to questioning in a way that reveals the good and everything else as well. As a reporting strategy, this approach is far more effective than the probing, even inquisitorial mode of some reporters. But it isn't a strategy, it's a way of looking at the world.

When we began working together on magazine pieces, I had no idea where it would lead, but in retrospect it was the perfect preparation for our work on books. I don't know that the editorial relationship we have is unique, but I have never encountered another like it. That we work together from the start of a project, from the inception of an idea, is a process that asks more from the author than it does from the editor. The author must set aside that natural self-protectiveness that any work in its early stages inspires. A "thick skin" doesn't begin to describe the necessary virtue. It is essentially an act of generosity. The editor needs only some tact and the willingness to read things repeatedly.

The advantages to this approach are vast. The editor has the satisfaction of being part of the conception of the work, and thus takes some responsibility for it, getting involved when there is time for influence. I don't consider much of my life to be exemplary, but this way of working is worth imitating for a writer and editor. It is not the easiest arrangement to come by, and in truth we simply fell into it through a meshing of personality and circumstance, and good fortune too—that is, an initial success, with Kidder's *The Soul of a New Machine.*

•

One frequently hears the complaint that "editors don't edit anymore." It is true that the publishing industry is not organized to reward editors who spend a lot of time on books that are under contract and will not appear for two or three or four years to come. In most houses, anyway, the pressure is to sign up something new and promising and to keep doing so (and to go to meetings about sales and marketing). In this sense editors resemble venture capitalists, their main task to find brightness and bring it to the public.

There are two kinds of pleasure for editors. One is acquisition, the collector's pleasure. The other is working with writers. It is like the difference between buying an antique car in mint condition or buying one that needs work. I am more the mechanic. (A strange thing to say, since I am incapable of fixing anything that isn't made of words.) But editors who collect and admire are often better than the mechanics at promoting their books. As a writer, of course, what you really want is someone strong on both counts.

If some editors don't really like to edit, it is equally true that writers themselves sometimes resist editing. I always wince when a reviewer says, "This book needed an editor." Often it had an editor, but the writer prevailed. Sometimes a book arrives at an editor's desk too late for the editor to make a substantial difference. The writer is exhausted and committed to his errors, the publishing schedule is set, it is simply too late all around. To repeat: a writer should try to involve the editor early in the process. If editors resist, well, there is not much you can do. You don't want a perfunctory involvement. You want investment.

I edit a distinguished man of science and medicine. Ignorant of much of his subject, learning every time I read his manuscripts, I nonetheless sometimes find myself in dispute with him about the internal logic of his arguments. Once he seemed to participate in a scientific fallacy that deems the understanding of a physical process superior to a moral or emotional understanding. If you can trace the neural pathways of criminality, do you know more about criminals than Dostoyevsky knows? No, you know something different. I accused my friend of "scientific triumphalism," a term that lives on between us. Editing at its best involves the intellectual engagement between editor and author.

Editing at its worst is more like combat. As a young magazine editor, I once worked with a ferocious investigative journalist, a man of great energies and passion, but also of innuendo, fact-stretching, and turgidity. This was an abject failure of mine. I don't remember many of the details, though I do remember getting drunk in a hotel room with his manuscript spread out on the bed, falling asleep, unable to fix it. Sometimes editing becomes a test of both intellect and character. I failed on both counts. I couldn't get the many problems of the manuscript straight in my own head and I couldn't face the fact that I couldn't solve them. Worse, I lacked the strength to confront him. Sometimes editors have to say: "Okay, I don't get it. Take me through this every step of the way." What I remember best is his describing his technique for getting a source to talk to him: "So I called him up and told his secretary, 'Okay, if he won't talk, just tell him I'm going to go with the fellatio story.'" This whole dreary episode yields little instruction for a writer, but an editor can learn plenty from it. You have to admit your confusion, and you have to go back to the author. You can't assume that you can fix what's wrong all by yourself.

How do people find their way into this business? I was once on a panel with another editor, who said the most extraordinary thing. Asked why she went into publishing, she said, "Well, I just really like writers."

Imagine liking writers! I mean liking writers as a class of people. Safecrackers or jugglers or dental hygienists, sure—but writers? Writers are by nature narcissists. In the clinical sense, that is, not the commonplace sense of "egotists." (They can be egotists too, but only once have I fallen asleep while listening to a writer on the telephone.) In a way, they have to be narcissists, at least while they are working. To maintain the concentration and self-belief necessary to see one's project as preeminently worthy generally requires a distorted sense of reality. It's as if you are required to think your work more important than it is in order to make it seem important at all. Perspective, a balanced view of life, is a virtue that tends to make one into agreeable company, but it can be death to a writer in the midst of a book.

Editing is a wifely trade. This is a disquieting thought for editors, certainly for male editors, and in a different way for some female editors too, but editing does involve those skills that are stereotypically female: listening, supporting, intuiting. And, like wives, editors are given to irony and indirection. When male editors become bullies it may be because they resent their feminized role. (They shouldn't take it out on writers. They need other avenues for their manly impulses, skydiving, Formula One racing, something.) However hesitant, timid, and self-doubting writers feel, they nonetheless remain the stereotypically male figures in the relationship, whatever their gender. Writers assert. Editors react.

Editors and writers need each other. Ultimately editors need writers more than the reverse, which is a wise thing for editors to keep in mind.

I have played both parts. I've been a writing editor—narcissist or helpmeet, depending on the day of the week. All editors take heart from T. S. Eliot's observation: "Some editors are failed writers, but so are most writers." To write can have a good or a bad influence on your editing. Being edited makes you more sensitive to the ways in which the editorial hand, so innocuous seeming when you are wielding it, can cause pain. On the other hand, if you think of yourself as a writer, you may too easily imagine that the answer to another writer's problem is your own fine prose.

Most of my writing (and a lot of my editing) has been done for magazines. I have worked for a couple of brilliant magazine editors whose genius lay not so much in editing line by line, but in conception and boldness—a willingness to trust the writer and to be surprised (even at the cost of surprising advertisers). The ordinary magazine experience, by contrast, can be dreary. The remark one doesn't want to hear from a magazine editor is, "We love your piece. We just have a few suggestions." This often means a total rewrite, and one they have already undertaken to do.

Editors, in any medium, should avoid rewriting, and if they do try to rewrite, then the writer is justified in resisting. Revision by an editor never works as well as when the writer does the work. If editors do add words, they should try to maintain the author's style and idiom, in the spirit of those signs you used to see at dry cleaners: "invisible reweaving." The surest way to do harm to a piece of writing is to impose one's own style on it.

Editors need a hierarchical sense of a manuscript, book, or article. They need to see its structure, its totality, before they become involved in minutiae. A writer should be on the alert when an editor starts by fixing commas or suggesting little cuts when the real problem resides at the level of organization or strategy or point of view. Most problems in writing are structural, even on the scale of the page. Something isn't flowing properly. The logic or the dramatic logic is off. Editors ideally can hear and see prose in a way that the writer cannot. And to notice may be enough, preferable to trying to fix it oneself. Sometimes you need only write "tone" next to a problematic passage for the author to hear it afresh and realize that it is sounding a sour note.

A sense of hierarchy is all the more necessary in editing because writers, too, want to concentrate on the little things. Writers, especially students, will sometimes say, "I can't wait until you mark up my manuscript." This sounds, as it's meant to sound, open and flexible. But I usually feel a bit trapped, even manipulated by this kind of remark. To take your pencil to a manuscript is to endorse it, to say it just needs "some fixes," when in fact it is just as likely to need rethinking altogether. I want to say, and sometimes do say, "Well, let's see if it's ready to be marked up."

Kidder, along with many writers, claims that the first draft is the hardest. I have never fully understood this. The first draft is the occasion to scatter all your bright notions on the page, without the awful limitations of finality, the facing-it recognition that what you've got is all there is. But perhaps it is a matter of the strictures you place on yourself, a matter of what you mean by a first draft. If it is more than an elaboration of notes, if it struggles for sequentiality, then yes, draft one can make you quail. Kidder, in one of the many head games he plays upon himself, has a capacity to pretend that his first draft is his final draft even though another part of his mind knows full well that it will be altered greatly, maybe even discarded.

Kidder has accused me of disingenuousness for always praising a first draft. It's true that initial praise is almost a reflex for me. But praise of the imperfect need not be insincere. In fact, it can sometimes be more sincere than the writer realizes, sincere in a different way. I may like not what I see but what I imagine. You have to envision the potential of a piece of writing, and potential can sometimes be more exciting than reality. Emily Dickinson's line "I dwell in possibility, a fairer house than prose" is an editor's motto.

No writer known to me revises so energetically and even enthusiastically as Kidder. It is a great gift to be able to consider your own work—hard wrought—as thoroughly provisional. Of the things we have learned in revising, perhaps the most important is the concept of sacrifice. Sometimes passages, even chapters, characters, or themes, that are perfectly good in themselves must go for the good of the whole.

All good writing ultimately is a contest with the inexpressible. Every good passage leaves something unsaid. So it ought to be hard. But you don't want to make it harder than necessary. The best thing an editor can do is to help the writer to think, and this is the most satisfying part of an editor's work, collaborating at the level of structure and idea.

The process that Kidder and I have worked out over the years has been a source of great comfort—for both of us, I think. The ritual of the final read-aloud has a particular significance. I know this is not a universal practice among writers and editors, and for understandable reasons. One approaches it with some apprehension. It is inevitably chastening. The writer cannot hide from the sound of his own voice, and writer and editor alike must encounter mistakes that have lurked in plain view all along, now suddenly blatant and full of reproach. And satisfying as it is to correct them at last, you know that some other blunder remains undiscovered. All books are imperfect. John Updike once wrote about his lifelong pleasure in receiving the first copy of a book of his from the publisher, a pleasure, he said, that lasts until you find the first typo. At some point in our proceedings Kidder will likely invoke Melville: "This whole book is draught—nay but the draught of a draught." And I may then chime in with my own favorite line from that passage: "God keep me from ever completing anything."

In the long course of a book and the longer course of a career, we have disagreed and even nettled each other from time to time (and done some eye rolling in private). But we have never exchanged an angry word. It helps, I suppose, that we were both raised to be polite. But we have also had our well-established roles.

Only recently have we experimented in reversing them.

Late in our association, after we had been working together for about thirty-five years, I wrote *The Thing Itself*, which claimed to be cultural criticism. It was that, but as it got closer to the end it became increasingly personal, part essay, part memoir. I gave Kidder the manuscript for his comments. He returned it a few days later, and I opened it to see his bold hand—large and legible, completely unlike the squiggly marks I tend to make—marching through the pages, leaving various messages, none of them wanting in candor. His most memorable advice was "Shit-can this." I was fully recovered within three weeks.

Subtler instruction did occur. For instance, I had written about something of which I had been "absurdly proud," something that it would have been absurd to be proud of, in fact. Kidder had circled "absurdly." I stared, then got it. I had been begging for the reader's sympathy. The adverb was asking forgiveness for what the adjective confessed. Out went "absurdly," and the sentence was stronger for it.

But it was not until we were deep into the present book that I felt the full otherworldly power of role reversal. Kidder was trying to cajole me into a piece of work, and he cited Keats's advice to Shelley on avoiding excesses: "Curb your magnanimity," wrote the tactful Keats. I had the opposite problem, in Kidder's view: stinginess. He was trying to make me flesh out a typically underdone paragraph of mine. "Unleash your magnanimity," he said.

Oh brother. It had come to this. One had heard oneself.

NOTES ON USAGE

In 1859 Ralph Waldo Emerson wrote: "Never use the word *development*. Dangerous words in like kind are *display, improvement, peruse, circumstances* . . ."

Those words have survived the great man's scorn—though he was probably right about "peruse." Every generation has its verbal fashions and critics who deplore them. Some usages, seemingly poisonous, get absorbed harmlessly into the language; others die out. A century after Emerson, many were alarmed by the spread of "finalize," but that epidemic subsided, and the word doesn't seem to cause much concern when it appears today. About the same time, "hopefully" (as in, "Hopefully, things will get better") sent critics into merry indignation. Strunk and White sniffed, "It is not merely wrong, it is silly." William Zinsser called it an "atrocity." It was said to be grammatically incorrect, a "misplaced modifier." In fact, in its disputed usage, "hopefully" serves as a sentence adverb, a word modifying an entire sentence, not necessarily the word it precedes. It functions no differently from "seriously," or "frankly." The unacknowledged objection to "hopefully" was social, a matter of taste. Sophisticated people just didn't like the sound of what was then a new usage, especially since unsophisticated people were using it with such apparent pleasure. Today, probably because of the opprobrium heaped on it, fewer people seem to use "hopefully," and even fewer seem to care.

It is tempting to despise all neologisms, but many of them simply reflect the constancy of change in the world. Here is a sentence from the news in 2011 that couldn't have been understood ten years earlier: "Christopher Lee, a second-term Republican from upstate New York, resigned after a disclosure by a Web site, Gawker.com, that he had sent embarrassing photographs and misrepresented himself to a woman he contacted through Craigslist." You can mourn for a world where companies were once named like mighty ships. Now they take names that sound like bath toys, such as Yahoo! or YouTube, but that's what they're called, and there's no way around it. To Google has entered the language, and it's precious to surround the word with ironic quotation marks.

English changes constantly. No sensible person would want it otherwise. But even if they do it silently, all writers and most readers simmer with distaste for certain words and phrases. We do this even as we acknowledge that today's outrage is tomorrow's shrug. Here are some usages, circa 2012, that we would happily expunge from the language.

- "Going forward." Sometime in the 1990s, many Americans of the corporate and professional classes seemed to grow tired of the phrase "in the future" (and "someday" or "soon" or "later on" or the unadorned future tense), and they started saying "going forward" instead. It may be here to stay, but it still carries a Panglossian tone, a faith in the five-year plan.

- "Proactive." This is a neologism and an annoying one. Even more annoying, it's a succinct way of naming a quality that otherwise takes a couple of words to express. It too seems to ally the writer with a world of committees and agendas, as do "stakeholder," "planful," "impactful."
- Certain nouns used as verbs: "parent," "access," "impact." Also nouns rejiggered into verbs—"incentivize," or just "incent," for instance.
- "Grow," as in "to grow one's business," deserves a category all its own. Why does it seem okay to grow corn and not an economy? Sheer prejudice, and we share it.
- Adjectives and adverbs suffering from exhaustion: "sustainable," "green," "iconic," "incredible" and "incredibly." The last two, like Chernobyl, should be out of service for decades to come. "Ironic" and "ironically" must be used reluctantly and not as labels for things that are merely odd. "Famously" ("As Yogi Berra famously said . . .") is just a tired way of excusing a tired reference.
- Phrases that once seemed fresh: "low-hanging fruit," "tipping point," "herding cats," "on steroids," "putting the toothpaste back in the tube," "at the end of the day," and "welcome to the world of . . ." (as a way of announcing the subject of a story after an anecdotal opener).
- Misused words: "Enormity" still means something horrible, not just anything big. "Fractious" means ill-behaved, not divisive. "Disinterested" (impartial) and "uninterested" (bored) are not synonyms, nor are "infer" and "imply."
- Phrases that seem to be in a transitional state and can no longer be used for fear of confusion: "Beg the question" was

once used as a criticism of a circular argument, but now can mean "makes you want to ask." Neither meaning can be assumed. "The proof is in the pudding" is an illogical phrase that exists only because of its history. If you use the original version, you sound quaint: "The proof of the pudding is in the eating." Something similar has happened to "couldn't care less," which has inexplicably devolved into the illogical "could care less." There is also the uncompleted "as far as," as in, "As far as geography, I think it's in Africa."

- Malapropisms: "free reign," "shoulder on," "tow the line," "perks your interest," "a tough road to hoe," "doesn't jive with the facts."

- Words whose main function is to call attention to themselves: e.g., "eponymous."

- Overused intensifiers: "preternatural," "quintessential," "epicenter."

- Journalistic adjectives: "top," "key," "leading," "ranking."

- Words invoking metaphorical places: "realm," "arena." Or words expressing big, vague numbers: "myriad," "light-years."

- Medical vulgarisms and clichés: "adrenaline" for energy, "testosterone" for masculinity, "anatomy" for body, and "cancer" for any bad thing that has "metastasized."

- Political clichés: "grassroots," "groundswell," "kicking the can down the road," "partisan bickering," "red meat," "playing to the base."

- "Folks" for people. Now used indiscriminately everywhere, but especially by public speakers stooping to an audience.

When a president says "folks like me," you are only reminded that there are no folks like him—he's the president. Other aggressively informal words: "most" for almost ("most everyone agrees"), "couple" as an adjective ("he drove for a couple miles").

- Words that proclaim one's own inability as a writer: "indescribable," "beyond words," "ineffable."
- Phrases from pop culture that come all too easily to a weary mind: "a little help from my friends," "make my day," "it's not over 'til it's over," "a perfect storm," "your fifteen minutes" (of fame), "it is what it is," "I'm just sayin'," "zip, zilch, nada" (and other cute ways of saying none). To realize how sad these expressions will look in print within a decade or so, consider some of their ancestors: "sock it to me," "fab," "dig it," "far out."
- Words and phrases of the digital age: "killer app," "reboot." Also "mega" and "giga" and "nano" as prefix-metaphors.
- The euphemism "pass" for "die." ("Pass away" was bad enough.)
- All sports metaphors.

Some Notes on Grammar

Like mangled phrases, grammatical errors gain legitimacy through widespread use, but more slowly, perhaps because they never stop offending the ears of those who learned to fear them in elementary school. Here are some that should still be avoided:

- "Between you and I." It is properly "between you and me," and the objective case is required in all such instances. ("They invited my wife and me to participate"; "It seems to Fred and me that we must . . .") Yes, Shakespeare makes the error in question (in *The Merchant of Venice*: ". . . all debts are clear between you and I"). But his precedent does not govern, not yet anyway.
- "I wish I would have . . ." This was once largely a regionalism (Midwest), but it is spreading. "I wish I had" is correct.
- Danglers. If nothing worse, danglers can be embarrassing. A prominent wine critic used to write sentences of this sort: "A dark, brooding, muscular claret with cigar box aromas and hints of cherries in the finish, I have never tasted a better offering from this chateau."
- Confusion between the verbs "lie" and "lay." Emerson was fighting the battle 150 years ago and nothing has changed. "Lie" is intransitive, "lay" transitive. "I lie down." "I lay my body down." Even in speech one should get this right. Remember Bob Dylan's lyric: "Lay, lady, lay, lay across my big brass bed." Remember it because it's wrong, even though sexier his way.
- Subjunctives. Beware the reflexive use of "were" after "if." Part of the confusion is that this use of "were" belongs to what was once an entire system of subjunctive constructions. Everyone knows that "were" is correct in such common usages as "If I were you," and "If it were up to me." But it is tempting to use "were" when it doesn't apply. In if-then constructions, "were" is now properly confined to statements contrary to fact or of doubtful truth. When expressing a

fact, do not use the subjunctive, not even when "if" is involved: "If it was going to cost me a thousand bucks, then damn it, I was going to enjoy it." Meaning that a thousand dollars was in fact the price. Most subjunctives are dead or dying and unnecessary. "Whether tomatoes be a fruit or a vegetable" has begun to sound affected, and is not required even in the most formal prose.

- Verb agreement. More and more, writers make the verb agree with the last noun rather than the true subject of the sentence. ("The issue of continued job losses haunt the administration." It has to be "haunts.")
- Gendered pronouns. In a few instances in this book we have followed the convention by which the masculine pronoun stands for both sexes. This practice is eroding fast, and with reason. Already the rule seems effectively to have changed for subjects that are singular in form but plural in meaning. "Everyone should do his best," we were taught to say. Or "Nobody knows his manners these days." In these cases the plural pronoun ("Everyone should do *their* best") avoids bias at no great cost to the language. The *New York Times* copy desk now allows this violation. In at least some other situations—for instance, an address to the graduating class of male and female firefighters—common decency endorses using the awkward "his or her."

In other cases requiring a singular pronoun, some writers change "he" to "she," whether consistently or alternately or randomly. This may have come to seem natural to those who do it, but to many readers (to us) it seems self-congratulatory. But then again, we are members of a generation that hears a stern voice in the ear enforcing the old rule. It is a weak defense to point out that the voice belongs to a woman who was teaching sixth grade.

Other solutions have been proposed. The conservative writer Charles Murray has an idea that is simplicity itself: use the pronoun appropriate to your own sex. (Jane says *everyone/her*; John says *everyone/his*. Unfortunately no one seems to recognize this rule except Charles Murray, and it costs him nothing to follow it since he is a man.

The language has yet to come up with a universally acceptable solution. In most cases it's possible to write around the problem, by making the subject plural or changing the sentence structure in some other way.

• "May" and "might." Avoid the troubling construction favored by sportscasters in which something that could have happened in the past is described as if perhaps it did happen: "If he'd caught that pass, they may have won the game." The past tense of "may" is "might."

• "Who" and "whom" confusion. In speech, one can always use "who" when in doubt. It is better to be informal and wrong than wrong and pompous. Common pompous errors: "Whom shall I say is calling?" "Give the job to whomever will do it better." The rule governing such constructions isn't altogether obvious. "Whom" is the objective case, but in phrases like the preceding ones the whole clause ("whoever will do it better") functions as the object, with "whoever" the subject of the clause. This rule may be arbitrary, but it is the rule, and violations of it grate on educated ears. In formal writing you don't want to be wrong *or* pompous, so it's worth taking time to figure it out. "Who shall I say is calling?" is correct, as is "The person whom you called is not in."

- "Which" and "that." Fastidious writers congratulate themselves on getting the distinction right, and the more libertine take at least as much pleasure in their ignorance. One ought to know the distinction and follow the rule without getting snooty about it. The crux of the matter is the difference between restrictive and nonrestrictive clauses. *Modern English Usage* explains it in more detail than almost anyone requires, but the passage is clear, definitive, and entertaining. See Fowler.

WRITING GUIDES AND REFERENCES: A SELECTIVE BIBLIOGRAPHY

The Artful Edit, by Susan Bell (Norton)

The Art of Time in Memoir, by Sven Birkerts (Graywolf Press)

The Writing Life, by Annie Dillard (Harper & Row)

Writing with Power, by Peter Elbow (Oxford University Press)

Writing Creative Nonfiction, edited by Carolyn Forché and Philip Gerard (Story Press)

Tough, Sweet and Stuffy, by Walker Gibson (Indiana University Press)

The Situation and the Story, by Vivian Gornick (Farrar, Straus and Giroux)

Intimate Journalism: The Art and Craft of Reporting Everyday Life, by Walt Harrington (Sage)

On Writing, by Stephen King (Scribner)

Telling True Stories, edited by Mark Kramer and Wendy Call (Plume)

Bird by Bird: Some Instructions on Writing and Life, by Anne Lamott (Pantheon)

The Forest for the Trees, by Betsy Lerner (Riverhead)

Unless It Moves the Human Heart, by Roger Rosenblatt (Ecco)

The Elements of Style, by William Strunk, Jr., and E. B. White (Macmillan)

Clear and Simple as the Truth, by Francis-Noel Thomas and Mark Turner (Princeton University Press)

Word Court, by Barbara Wallraff (Harcourt)

Style, by Joseph M. Williams and Gregory G. Colomb (Longman)

On Writing Well, by William Zinsser (Harper & Row)

The Chicago Manual of Style, by University of Chicago Press staff (University of Chicago Press)

Modern English Usage, by H. W. Fowler, revised edition by Sir Ernest Gowers (Oxford University Press)

Modern American Usage, by Wilson Follett (Hill and Wang)

Words into Type, by Marjorie E. Skillin and Robert M. Gay (Prentice-Hall)

ACKNOWLEDGMENTS

We wish to thank Kate Medina, Betsy Lerner, Georges Borchardt, and Chris Jerome for their generosity, enthusiasm, and guidance. We are grateful to Anna Pitoniak, Evan Camfield, and London King of Random House, and to the writers Stuart Dybek, Tom French, Darcy Frey, Diane Hume George, Pamela Haag, Michael Janeway, Suzannah Lessard, Michael Ponsor, and Barbara Wallraff. Above all, we owe thanks to our families for their patience and wisdom.

INDEX

ABOUT THE AUTHORS

―――――――

TRACY KIDDER graduated from Harvard and studied at the University of Iowa. He has won the Pulitzer Prize, the National Book Award, the Robert F. Kennedy Award, and many other literary prizes. The author of *Strength in What Remains, My Detachment, Mountains Beyond Mountains, Home Town, Old Friends, Among Schoolchildren, House,* and *The Soul of a New Machine,* Kidder lives in Massachusetts and Maine.

RICHARD TODD has been a magazine and book editor for more than forty years. He was executive editor of *The Atlantic Monthly* and published books under his own imprint at Houghton Mifflin. He has contributed reportage and cultural criticism to a number of magazines, and is the author of *The Thing Itself.* He has taught at Amherst and Smith colleges and the University of Massachusetts; currently he is on the faculty of the Goucher College MFA program.

ABOUT THE TYPE

In 1931 Monotype made this facsimile of the typeface cut originally for John Bell by Richard Austin in 1788, using as a basis the matrices in the possession of Stephenson Blake & Co. Used in Bell's newspaper, "The Oracle," it was regarded by Stanley Morison as the first English Modern face. Although inspired by French punchcutters of the time, with a vertical stress and fine hairlines, the face is less severe than the French models and is now classified as Transitional. Essentially a text face, Bell can be used for books, magazines, long articles, et cetera.